MW00653767

GOLDEN DAWN

By

Peter B. Kyne

COSMOPOLITAN BOOK CORPORATION

NEW YORK, 1930

TO

KATHLEEN JOHNSON

GOLDEN
DAWN

GOLDEN DAWN

CHAPTER ONE

M R. THEODORE GATLIN'S married life had
demonstrated to him the absolute fallacy of the
ecclesiastic contention that marriages are made in
heaven.

In the beginning he had married Louise Hanchett for
a number of reasons, none of them really important.
She was of good family; i.e., her parents were prosperous middle-class folk whom scandal had never
touched. They were eminently respectable if a trifle
bovine in disposition, and Louise was their only child,
and sole heir to such worldly goods as her parents
might have accumulated and which Mr. Gatlin believed they were not likely to dissipate; for which
reason he did not contemplate having to support them
in their helpless old age.

These were the common-sense reasons which his self-
respect as a business man indicated he should conjure
to his defense in making this important step; in reality
they were merely a sop to his real reason for the step,
which was a mad infatuation he mistook for love.
Louise Hanchett's cold, classical beauty and Vere de

Vere form, which she knew how to dress beautifully and in good taste, had so dazzled him that it never occurred to him to ask himself whether the object of his passion had wearing qualities; if she had common sense; if she was healthy and capable of bearing children; if she was of sound ancestry. However, there was some excuse for this carelessness in Mr. Gatlin's case, as, indeed, there is in the case of all but supermen. Engaged as he was in the retail shoe business, he had never heard of Mendel's law, and if anybody, in conversation with him, had mentioned genetics, he would doubtless have thought that they were some new form of athletic contrivance. The only practical information he had on the Hanchett family was that Mrs. Hanchett was a shrew, that Mr. Hanchett was a middle-aged man whose head was bloody and bowed; that Louise was unhappy at home.

In Mr. Gatlin the protective instinct, abundant in all males, was particularly well-developed; so he yearned to provide Louise with the happiness he knew she had missed and which he, thank God, was able to provide— for he had also the usual amount of masculine ego.

Following two years of married life, during which he strove manfully to accomplish the impossible, Mr. Theodore Gatlin went into a mental haze. Six months of this and he became peevish. He wanted a child— and when at last he realized that, in the phraseology of his times, there was nothing doing, there was born in him the first coherent thought he had ever had on the subject of matrimony. He told himself that he was sick unto death striving to be a good husband and acquiring no merit because of his efforts. He told himself he had a house but not a home; that Louise had "taken after her mother," which meant that he had taken after his afflicted father-in-law!

He gave considerable thought to the subject and finally decided that Louise would be all right if she only had something to occupy her mind. She sought happiness and blamed him because she could not find it. Mr. Gatlin did not know where happiness might be found, but inasmuch as he was moderately certain of peace of mind while attending to his business, he had a hazy impression that happiness is not infrequently found in securing a job and working at it. Unfortunately he knew of no job at which Louise might reasonably be expected to function well, unless it might be that of mothering a baby; so when a physician informed him that his hopes of fatherhood were not apt to be realized, he had a brilliant idea and broached it to Mrs. Gatlin.

"Let's adopt a baby!" he urged.

Louise demurred. She had her doubts as to the advisability of taking over somebody's else troubles— one never knew how an adopted baby was going to turn out—there was no hurry anyhow—she must have time to consider the idea—her health.

"To hell with your health!" Mr. Gatlin roared, for the first time in his married life becoming vulgar.

"Every doctor you've had tells me you're organically sound. You only think you're sick."

"My nerves," she protested, but he silenced her.

"You think too much about yourself and not at all about anybody else, particularly me. What you need is a baby to fuss with. You'll learn to love it in a month as much as if it was your own flesh and blood."

"I'm afraid you'll not love it, Theodore. You're so cranky and irritable," she defended.

"Listen!" Mr. Gatlin commanded. "I'm at the point where I'm seriously considering suing you for divorce on the grounds that you're a barren woman. In other ways you don't measure up to my idea of a wife and companion. It's no fun for me to come home night after night and have to listen to your tales of woe—"

"You are devoid of sympathy," his wife charged. "You neglect me."

"Maybe I've failed," said Mr. Gatlin, "but, by jiminy, I've tried, and I'm willing to keep on trying a little longer. Only from now on, we're going to try my methods, and adopting a baby is one of them. If that fails I'll take the baby over myself and we'll call in the lawyers."

She knew she had gone as far as she dared. Even the dullest of married women know when that point is reached; that is, they know when it has been reached for that day.

"Well, if we can find a baby of good, sound, intelligent, healthy parentage," she assented grudgingly.

"I've got one staked out," Mr. Gatlin cried joyfully, "and I know its parents. They're sound as grindstones. I know the grandparents of the child on both sides.

"I don't know them personally," he went on, "but I've had a doctor look up their records. High-class people. No insanity and no crookedness in them."

"I'll have to meet these grandparents and parents, Theodore."

"Unfortunately," he replied, "they're all dead."

"What did they die of?"

"The grandparents on both sides of old age; the father of the baby was an army captain and he got killed in a fight in the Sulu Islands. The mother died in childbirth and the baby is in the Infants' Shelter in San Francisco. No record of relatives—and the child is up for adoption."

"Boy or girl, Theodore?"

"Boy."

"I could never stand a boy, Theodore. I must have a girl."

Mr. Gatlin grinned evilly. "I figured you'd try to edge out of it that way. It isn't a boy. It's a girl."

"Are you certain it is a legitimate baby?"

"I'm morally certain she is, but what if she isn't? I've satisfied myself as to her breeding, and that's all that matters. The mother of one of our greatest Americans was illegitimate—and a mighty good thing it was for that greatest of our Americans. That illicit cross gave him an infusion of the blood of a gentleman and it made him great. His mother's stock was ordinary. The doctor told me all about it," he added parenthetically.

Louise Gatlin was not very intelligent, but she was sufficiently so to realize that for once in his life Mr. Gatlin was due to have his own way.

That night as he lay abed, Mr. Gatlin suddenly gave himself a prodigious poke in the ribs. "What a jackass I was not to consult that doctor before I married Louise," he groaned. "When I thought I could father a child of my own I didn't pay any more attention to its ancestry than I would to selecting a necktie. Anything that looked well would fill the bill. But when it came to selecting some other man's baby, I gave the job all the attention I would give to the purchase of a piece of property. I wouldn't think of buying a lot until I had run down the record of the title and satisfied myself there were no flaws in it. If men would only employ that much common sense in selecting their wives—or wives, in selecting their husbands! I knew what a nervous, complaining, selfish old shrew her mother was—what's that law the doctor spoke of? Ah, yes. Mendel's law. The law that like shall produce like. Simple! Natural! Any fool should have thought of that—and yet it took an old monk—a celibate—to promulgate the news. Whew-w-w-w!"

"Theodore," said his wife, from the other twin bed, "I should think you might be more considerate of me than to whistle like that and wake me up."

"I'm so happy, dear, I couldn't help it. Forgive me."

"Have you thought of a name for the baby?"

"I have. Penelope."

"A horrid name. Where under heaven did you get that name?"

To her unspeakable amazement he quoted a verse from Henry Herbert Knibbs's poem, "Out There Somewhere":

"We'll dance a merry saraband from here to
    drowsy Samarkand;
Along the sea, across the land, the birds are
    flying south,
And you, my sweet Penelope, out there some-
    where you wait for me,
With buds of roses in your hair and kisses on
    your mouth."

They went by train to San Francisco next day. Accompanied by the doctor who had accouched the child's mother, they went to the Infants' Shelter and claimed the baby. With the child in his arms and accompanied by his wife and the lady manager of the Infants' Shelter, Mr. Gatlin repaired to the Superior Court of the City and County of San Francisco, and legally adopted the daughter of Captain Ronald Elliot and Janet Elliot, both deceased.

From the court-room they went to Grace Cathedral and had her baptized in the Episcoplian faith—out of courtesy to Mrs. Gatlin's latest religious crotchet, Mr. Gatlin having no religious affiliations whatsoever. There was a slight hitch here. The pastor had just sprinkled water on the little dark head and said: "I baptize thee in the name of the Father, and of the Son, and of the Holy Ghost, and give thee the name of—" when Mrs. Gatlin interrupted softly—"Lucretia."

"Nothing doing," Mr. Gatlin declared. "Lucretia! Wasn't that the woman that poisoned people—a wop woman? Her name shall be Penelope. I like that name."

The pastor smiled faintly. Having already sensed that all of the enthusiasm for the child was Mr. Gatlin's, he was seized with a perverse desire to please the sentimental fellow, so he said quickly: "—and give thee the name of Penelope."

Mr. Gatlin hugged Penelope to him and kissed her back of the left ear, an act inspired by his childishness and childlessness, plus his protective instinct.

"You mustn't kiss her, Theodore," his wife protested. "Kissing is insanitary. You might give her some sort of disease."

"Oh, lord," Mr. Gatlin murmured, "will I never cease making hideous mistakes?"

For in that illuminating instant he realized that in adopting Penelope he had made a terrible mistake. His wife didn't want her! At the very moment of the commencement of his experiment he knew it was a failure. However, it was no part of his wife's intention (at least for the present) that he should realize this, so she took the baby from him, and sat down in a pew while Mr. Gatlin went into the pastor's study to get the baptismal certificate.

"I do hope, Mr. Gatlin," said the pastor, "that your adopted daughter will bring new joy into your married life. You have done a wonderful thing, a noble thing, a fine, Christian thing, and God will reward you for your great charity. You're a good man."

"I'm a damned fool," Mr. Gatlin replied ungraciously. "The poor little tot isn't going to get any better break than I've had."

Within the week, Theodore Gatlin, having communicated with the adjutant general of the army at Washington ascertained that Captain Ronald Elliot's body had been brought home from the Island of Sulu and interred in the National Cemetery at the Presidio of San Francisco. So he had Penelope's mother disinterred from the Potter's Field and reinterred beside the soldier, after which he gave orders for the erection of a suitable monument over them.

Viewing him from every angle, he was a most peculiar retail shoe dealer.

For a month all went well with the Gatlins, and then Mrs. Gatlin issued her fiat.

"Theodore," she said, "I must insist on one thing. Penelope must never know that you and I are not her natural parents. I feel that such knowledge might detract from her love for us."

"That won't work any hardship on me, my dear," he replied. "I feel just as enthusiastic about her as if I were her real father. Strange how a person can learn to love a strange child so quickly. I suppose it's because they're so helpless."

"Another thing, Theodore. I love Penelope dearly, as you know, but I can't be made a slave to her. Do you realize, dear, how she keeps me tied down?"

He gritted his teeth, and his wife went on: "We simply must have a nurse for her."

"Have two of 'em," he growled. "Whatever she needs she shall have."

"That's right. Start spoiling her immediately."

It was always like that. However, as the child developed, she brought Mr. Gatlin each day closer to happiness than he had ever been before. She was his refuge. She was a healthy baby and hence a happy baby, and there was not the slightest chance that she would ever be spoiled by having her own wishes perennially deferred to. If Louise Gatlin accomplished nothing else worth while (and this she accomplished unconsciously) she did nothing to inflate Penelope's ego, which, as everybody knows, is the breeding ground of human selfishness, which, in turn, accounts for the unhappiness of most of humanity. Mr. Gatlin, of course, would have undone, in secret, much of this good work, had not the realization come to him quite early in Penelope's little girlhood that any demonstration of excessive affection on his part was inevitably counteracted by an excessive severity on the part of his wife toward the child.

She was a pretty child of olive complexion, with

very dark blue eyes and rich, shiny, jet-black hair. She was unusually intelligent and affectionate, of quick sympathy and winning, gracious ways. She was the apple of Mr. Gatlin's eye, and by the time she was ten years old he no longer cared a snap of his finger for his wife.

If Penelope was Mr. Gatlin's refuge, he also was hers. She never complained to him—doubtless because she feared her foster-mother, who had succeeded in inculcating in the child a duty complex quite out of proportion to the lady's deserts. Nevertheless it was understood between them that they were a pair of outlaws; mutual sympathy drew them closer together each day; their mutual love was a sweet and holy sentiment.

Mrs. Gatlin's nerves did not improve through the years, although when Penelope was ten years old, a wandering evangelist came to town and commenced a furious campaign of conversion and curing by prayer every disease that flesh is heir to; and Mrs. Gatlin became "converted," prayed loudly, was prayed for loudly, and finally mounted the platform and shrieked: "Halleluiah, praise the lord! I'm cured."

And she was—until the local glamour of the miracle wore off and the evangelist moved on to other fields. Thereafter, life for Mr. Gatlin and Penelope became almost unbearable. She exhorted them to sorrow for their sins, and when Mr. Gatlin declared they hadn't any worth bothering about (which was quite true) she prayed for them. They had grace before and after meals, with family prayers and readings from the Bible. Sunday was a day of sorrow. Finally the worm turned.

In a moment of insane fury, Mr. Gatlin performed what he considered a long-neglected duty. He took Mrs. Gatlin's classical countenance in both hands, bumped her head repeatedly against the wall and told her that if she ever opened her mouth again in his presence without his permission he'd just about kill her. She didn't. She sued him for divorce and had Penelope on the witness stand to prove that Mr. Gatlin had beaten her; that he had remained away from home until late at night and refused to reveal his rendezvous. Mr. Gatlin entered a cross-complaint and petitioned to have Penelope allocated to him.

Unfortunately the judge was a pudding-head. He refused to accept Mr. Gatlin's explanation that he had laid hands on Mrs. Gatlin but once, and then only in a moment of frenzy. But he did not state where he had been in the habit of spending his evenings so suspiciously. He couldn't afford to. He was a prominent business man. However, the judge should have known. Probably he did, but even so he was unsympathetic. He granted Mrs. Gatlin the divorce, liberal alimony and the custody of Penelope; whereupon the honorable court was treated to the spectacle of Mr. Gatlin and Penelope weeping in each other's arms. However, Mr. Gatlin was permitted to have Penelope to himself two Sunday afternoons in each month and one-half of each school vacation.

The first Sunday afternoon Mr. Gatlin availed himself of this privilege, his quondam spouse had hysterics,
for with the malevolence of a devil Mr. Gatlin' announced he was taking Penelope to a ball game. He
took her, too, and they had a gorgeous time together
until a home run sailed into the bleachers and struck
Penelope violently on her pretty little nose. Mr. Gatlin,
with the unconscious form in his arms, fled to a hospital, where he was foolish enough to telephone Mrs.
Gatlin what had occurred. She appeared on the scene
and carried the child home at once.

Mr. Gatlin knew what she was up to. She was going
to cure Penelope's fractured nose by prayer—and he
had no faith in such therapy. He followed with a doctor, demanding at the front door to be admitted—a request which was ignored. So he kicked in the panels of
the front door, which he had no business to do because
it was no longer his, Mrs. Gatlin having acquired it in
the property settlement. Thereupon she summoned the
police by telephone and had him arrested, and the next
morning he was tried, found guilty and placed under
bond of a thousand dollars to remain away from the
place for one year.

He didn't do it, because he knew what would happen to Penelope if he did. And he could afford a thousand dollars—fifty thousand dollars, if need be—to
prevent that! He attacked within twenty-four hours—
at night, but he was quiet about it. He remembered he
had never surrendered his latch-key, so he entered
quietly and kidnaped Penelope.

Within two hours he was arrested en route to a San Francisco hospital in a motorcar with Penelope. For disobeying the magistrate, he was adjudged guilty of contempt of court, his bond of a thousand dollars was forfeited—and he was sentenced to sixty days in the county jail. Mrs. Gatlin preferred a charge of kidnaping against him, which is a felony, and since Mr. Gatlin knew he would be tried on that charge when he emerged from jail, he improved the shining hours by swearing to a warrant charging Mrs. Gatlin with insanity. Promptly she was brought before a board of alienists who declared her sane, and in order to avoid investigation into Mr. Gatlin's charge that she was denying Penelope medical attention, she turned her house over to an agent and disappeared—with Penelope.

From his cell in the county jail, Mr. Gatlin issued orders to his attorneys to find Penelope and take legal steps to prevent his ex-wife from removing her again beyond the jurisdiction of the court that had granted their divorce. A diligent search of three months failed of its object, so Mr. Gatlin neglected to deposit any alimony to his ex-wife's credit. He knew she could manage very well without the alimony. But he also knew Louise. She would have what was coming to her or know the reason why.

When six months had passed, Mr. Gatlin decided he had never been acquainted with her, for she failed to make any demand upon him for her alimony; hence he realized she preferred, by keeping Penelope from him, to cause him the maximum of suffering rather than reveal her whereabouts by making claim for the alimony due her. A year and a day from the date of the granting of her interlocutory decree, her attorneys petitioned for the final decree, which was granted. Mr. Gatlin then discovered she was living in Paris.

This news brought him no comfort. She was beyond reach of United States law, since, in departing from the state with Penelope, she had merely disobeyed an order of the court which instructed her to surrender Penelope to Mr. Gatlin from noon until seven p. m. two Sundays in each month. And contempt of court was not an extraditable offense. However, he had detectives place her under surveillance. They reported her as living alone, so Mr. Gatlin concluded she had placed Penelope in a school.

One day the detective agency sent him a very good kodak photograph of a little girl and asked him if this was the child he was seeking. The agency was unable to recognize in her the original of the photographs he had sent them.

When Mr. Gatlin gazed upon that photograph, he wept. Mrs. Gatlin's faith cure, as he had suspected it would, had proved wholly ineffective. In his agony, the words of the poem came back to him:

> "And you, my sweet Penelope, out there
>   somewhere you wait for me,
> With buds of roses in your hair and kisses
>   on your mouth."

He sold his retail shoe business and placed all of his
assets in a trust fund, the income to be paid to him
during his lifetime and to Penelope after his death.
He saved out of this trust fund, however, ten thousand dollars, with which he purchased a letter of credit
and a ticket to Cherbourg.

In the interim Mr. Gatlin's detectives had ascertained
that Penelope was in a school in Switzerland; he
planned to go to that school, abduct Penelope, and—his
plans were a trifle hazy, but he intended to mature them
as he crossed the Atlantic. Once in possession of Penelope, he would see to it that she should never know unhappiness again, if any effort of his could prevent it.
He was worth half a million dollars—half in cash and
the remainder in real estate that was rapidly appreciat-
ing in value. He could afford to retire. They would go
somewhere and lose themselves.

En route to the station—the first leg of his journey
—the automobile in which he was riding was struck
by another car and turned over. Mr. Gatlin was thrown
out and suffered a basal fracture of the skull, from
which he died six hours later.

CHAPTER TWO

STEPHEN BURT, M. D., was the sort of man whose waiting-room always would have been crowded, even if he had not been one-quarter as capable as his colleagues knew him to be. He was a man of sweet simplicity, absolute honesty, and overwhelming sympathy; in short, he possessed the ideal personality for a successful physician.

Miss Lanning was his office nurse. In training schools for nurses—at least it was so in the hospital where Miss Lanning was trained—nurses and interns develop the sort of democracy and comradeship which delights in nicknames—and in dispensing with formality. Quite early in her professional career, therefore, Miss Lanning became known as Lanny. She was a not very good-looking, but capable, tremendously intelligent, forceful, driving person; exactly the type that would inevitably become an old maid.

When Lanny was thirty years old and Stephen Burt was sixteen, she had him for a patient. He had measles. "What a nice, well-mannered boy!" she thought, the first day. "What a dear lad!" she reflected the second day. "What a good, considerate patient!" she exclaimed to the doctor on the third day. "He must have had a sweet, sensible mother."

17

"Perhaps," the doctor had replied. "I never knew her and neither did the boy. She died at his birth. He's man-raised. His father is an old friend and patient of mine."

"Has he a stepmother?" Even then, Lanny realized she would be the victim of a pang of jealousy if the doctor answered in the affirmative, for already the boy had aroused her maternal instinct. She was relieved to learn that his father had foisted no such trial upon the boy.

On the fourth day of his illness she called him "dearie." On the fifth day, when she proffered him castor oil, for which he had the customary juvenile horror, he rebelled; but when Lanny said, "Now, darling, I'll feel badly if you refuse to obey me," the boy had been instantly contrite.

"I'm sorry, Lanny," he apologized. "I'm a pig to oppose you." And then he groaned and took it—and Lanny kissed him and wanted to weep over him because he was such a dear and hadn't any mother—not even a stepmother!

"Lanny," he said to her on the seventh day, "do you know I love you a lot? I wish dad would marry you, so you could be with me all the time."

Lanny's heart swelled with the poignant grief of her baffled maternity at that honest boyish avowal.

On the eighth day he developed double pneumonia, as a sequela to the measles. He almost died—and so did Lanny. The doctor swore—and so did Stephen's father—that nothing but Lanny's devoted nursing brought him through. She wept the day she realized if she drew another day's salary as his nurse, she would be accepting money under false pretenses; and she wept on two counts. First, because she was leaving Stephen, and second, because Stephen's father insisted on being too grateful for her services.

"There is a reward due you, Miss Lanning," he told her, "over and beyond the trifling remuneration given you in exchange for your devoted services. That's a debt Steve and I can never repay, but the boy thinks we ought to make a pretense at payment and so do I." He opened her hand-bag and slipped in an envelope.

When she got back to the nurses' home where she lived between calls, she discovered he had given her five thousand dollars! Young Stephen had already given her his photograph, endorsed: "To my dear Lanny, with love from Steve."

Nursing is the most personal and impersonal profession in this world. Lanny never expected to see Stephen Burt again, but she sent him at Christmas a four-ounce Fairy fishing rod from Hardy's in London. It cost her a month's wages. She knew his father was a fishing enthusiast and would probably inculcate the same enthusiasm in his boy. Steve had sent her roses on her birthday; and his love, by telegraph, Christmas eve, together with an exquisite little watch to replace the dollar timepiece she used to count pulse-beats. On New Year's Day, a year later, he made a formal call and she was out on a case; so the day she was relieved she called upon him.

"Hello, Lanny," he said—and kissed her. "I wanted to see you to get some advice. Do you think, Lanny, that I'd make a half decent doctor?"

"God made you for a doctor," Lanny assured him. "You'll not have to be more than a mediocre doctor to be financially successful. You were born with the ideal personality."

"Thanks, Lanny. I want to be a doctor, but I want to be a good one, too, so you tell me what I am to do about it. I've just graduated from high school. Made the honor roll," he confided shyly.

"How far up the honor roll?" Lanny's query had almost a fierce quality in it.

"Number one."

"And you were out of school two months of your last term. I'm proud of you, Stevie."

"Where shall I go to college, Lanny?"

"Where do you intend to practice when you're a doctor, Stevie?"

"Right here, in San Francisco."

"In that event you should attend a local university. You'll go to Stanford University," Lanny decided. "If you graduate with honor there you're bound to get an internship in Stanford University Hospital. About two years of that and you'll know what you want to specialize in, so off you'll go for a postgraduate course in Berlin, Vienna, and London for four years. Then you'll return, and I'll be your office nurse and manager. How's that for a program?"

"Just dandy, Lanny."

"It means ten years of grind, Stevie, but don't let time frighten you," she warned anxiously. "Once you know what you know and know that you know it, others will not be long discovering it also, and you'll be years ahead of the half-baked medical dunces this world is cursed with."

He flattered her immensely by taking her to luncheon and the matinée.

For the next four years Lanny did not see her boy, but he wrote her and remembered her at Christmas and on her birthdays. He did not disappoint her, however; he was an honor graduate from the Leland Stanford Junior Medical School and, true to Lanny's prediction, he was immediately given an internship at the university hospital in San Francisco. Inasmuch as Lanny frequently had patients at that hospital, they met several times a year. Lanny kept her ear to the ground, harkening to reports of his progress from worth-while sources, and learned that he was regarded as a young doctor of distinct promise.

One day, after he had been two years an intern, they met in the corridor. "I've been wanting to see you, Stevie," Lanny began without any preliminary fencing. "You've had your two years as an intern, and now it's time for your postgraduate course in Europe."

"Impossible, Lanny. My father has had a frightful reversal of fortune. He's done a father's full duty by me, and I'm not going to graft off him and perhaps sacrifice him in his old age. I'm self-supporting now and even saving a little from my salary. In a few years I shall be able to afford a modest office and go in for general practice."

"You've followed my program thus far and you'll continue until it's finished," Lanny announced. "I'll loan you the money. The five thousand dollars your father gave me has grown to seventy-five hundred dollars—and I've saved two thousand more, so I'm going to bank you, and you shall pay me six per cent on the money you borrow, and secure me by life insurance." She was thoughtful for a few moments. "Well, perhaps three years abroad will benefit you more than four years would an ordinary man. So we'll cut the program to three years. After all, you must have some comforts; you've got to live like a gentleman. You will resign here today and I'll have the money for you tomorrow."

"Oh, Lanny, you dear old sport, I can't do that!"

Thereupon Lanny struck him in a vital spot. Her stern and lonely soul was touched. Not often did she indulge herself in the weakness of tears, but they flooded her eyes now, and her breast heaved.

He was always touched at the sight of suffering; the vast underlying sympathy in his nature would never have it otherwise. Abruptly she left him! She knew he would seek her out later, to protest at greater length, to avow himself her eternal debtor for the offer and again decline it.

He called upon her at her lodgings that night—and Lanny won. It was a hard battle, but when Lanny, so to speak, lowered her head and went in to win, usually she succeeded.

Well, she had her way, and when he returned from Europe she had an office ready for him. She would be forty years old on her next birthday, and after eighteen years of the drudgery of private nursing she looked forward to her position in Stephen Burt's office with pleasurable anticipation.

She met him at the ferry depot, and he took her to his heart and kissed her five times—twice on each cheek and once on the lips. "Well, old pal," he said almost immediately, "I'm a specialist. Neurologist and psychiatrist, and you're to be my first patient. I must go over you thoroughly and see what makes you act the way you do."

Success was his. Modest at first, of course, but of rapid growth, and Lanny knew why. His patients fell in love with him and advertised him to their friends.

In two years Stephen Burt had repaid Lanny with interest; the third year he moved into new, sunny, roomy, and beautifully furnished offices, with a waiting-room as large as all of his previous offices had been. He joined the best club in town; he joined a country club and resolutely Lanny drove him out of the office on Wednesday and Saturday afternoons to play golf. She denied him the privilege of naming his own fees because she knew they would be too modest; she kept his free list to a minimum; knowing all his friends, she supervised his social duties; she kept his books and was a very devil of a collector; she wrote all his business letters and signed them for him; she invested his money for him, and since she was no mean psychologist, she could read a woman patient as she would a book. She was his Admirable Crichton, and he rewarded her with his confidence, his affectionate friendship, and a perfectly dazzling salary raise each Christmas.

He always kissed her at six o'clock on the twenty-fourth day of December in each year, for the five years preceding the late winter afternoon when Mr. Daniel McNamara called in behalf of the strangest patient Lanny's boy had ever been asked to accept.

CHAPTER THREE

IT had been a long, hard day. Dr. Burt was tired, and a Mrs. Rudolph Merton, who was rich and idle, not very intelligent and hence neurasthenic, had been fatiguing him with a recital of her imaginary aches, pains, and megrims.

He pressed a button under the desk, tapping out a code message to Lanny, and waited patiently, his glance on the door leading into her office. He knew she would appear momentarily and say: "I'm sorry, Dr. Burt, but Professor Finnegan has just telephoned that you are fifteen minutes late to your engagement to meet the great German savant, Herr Doktor Ufflitz."

To his distress and amazement Lanny did not appear. He waited three minutes and sent another code message to Lanny, adding the word "Help!" Still Lanny did not appear, so he said with his disarming smile: "Mrs. Merton, the five o'clock whistle has blown, and I can't listen to another word. I've just remembered a most pressing engagement, so now if you do not go at once I shall have to throw you out."

He had her by the arm and out the door before she could think of another symptom. Then he locked the door, pulled out the telephone plug, sat down in his swivel chair, put both legs up on his desk and loaded and lighted his pipe, just as the door to his nurse's office opened and Lanny said:

"I'm so sorry, but Professor Finnegan—"

"She's gone. Where did you go, leaving me here to suffer?"

"I was in the waiting-room, placating an insistent visitor. I told him you had gone for the day, but he wanted to come into your office and make certain. He flashed some sort of police badge at me, said he wasn't nutty and that his business was private."

"Whenever you admit a person whose business is private and personal I am called upon for mental and physical effort, *sans* a fee, Lanny. I'm tired."

"What you need, dearie," said Lanny, "is a nice, long, cool, Bourbon whisky highball."

"And while you're on the job, get me one too," a deep voice spoke from the door behind her.

"It's that police person," Lanny cried.

"It is," the police person agreed without malice, "and even if I am a cop I'm too smart to be fooled by the fibs of any woman. How are you, doc?"

"Tired," he murmured. "Worn to a razor edge talking sanely to the insane and the semi-insane, the subnormal and the abnormal. You appear sane, officer. Are you?"

"I'd be afraid to take a bet I am, doc. I handle my share o' nuts, too, and there's times they make me think I'm bugs instead o' them. My name's Dan McNamara and I'm the chief of police."

"Sit down, chief. No, not that chair. That's for nervous patients. It's an invention of the devil and helps to
shorten their visits and, consequently, their tales of
woe. Drag over that armchair." He smiled at Lanny
and held up two fingers.

That smile melted her. It always did. For five years
she had been trying to bully him, and his smile had
always defeated her, for which reason she often had
a brainstorm and threatened to resign his service. And
she would have done it, too, for she was a forceful
woman, only for the fear that he might replace her
with a nurse who didn't understand him—a la-de-la
young thing, half-baked professionally, who would fall
in love with him and make him marry her. He was so
kind and sympathetic Lanny knew he would marry her,
just to keep her from feeling badly.

"Damn his sympathy," she growled, as she prepared
the drinks in an inner room. "That's why he's worked
to death. He'll die young—overwork—angina, the
young fool! They all go that way. There—I've dropped
a tear in one of the highballs. Well, never mind, that
big, fresh, heavy-footed cop can swallow one of my
tears if he can't swallow one of my lies. How dare he
force his way in—the big bum! And getting a drink
for his dirty work! And that poor, patient dear just
settled for a quiet smoke."

She sniffled and served the highballs.

"You're mighty sweet, Lanny," Dr. Burt told her.
"Now, run along home."

Lanny did not go. She knew that big moocher of a chief of police would praise such old liquor and his host would offer him a second helping. So she sat in her office. In ten minutes she would look in on them again.

"I've got a girl down at Central Station," Dan McNamara was saying. "Shoplifting detail picked her up in a department store where she'd pinched a dozen and a half silk stockings. Petit larceny and caught with the goods. I sent a good man around to try to square the case with the department-store people, but they insist on pressing the charge, and that's too bad because she's got a couple of priors against her. Out on probation— suspended sentence, you understand, doc. And now she'll do two years in the Big House. 'S tough on the girl."

"What's your interest in her, if she's a confirmed thief?"

"Well, maybe she wouldn't be a thief if she'd had the breaks," he defended. "Somebody must have given her a sweet bust on the nose, because her beak's been broke and nothing's left of it but a saddle."

"Is she tough?"

"Is she tough? Doc, she's so tough I know it ain't natural. A girl as tough as her must be loony. But there ain't nothing tough about her eyes or her mouth —and that's where you can always find toughness that's been bred in the bone. There's something about this girl that's different, doc. I don't know what it is but I know this much: she wasn't always tough. I want you to give her the once-over."

"I understand there is a psychologist and psychiatrist —Dr. Blethen—who does all of the medico-legal work for the department, chief. I wouldn't care to examine the girl except on his invitation."

"Yes, I know. Question of ethics, and while the question is being debated this girl gets hauled into court and takes the rap on the old charge of grand theft. I know Blethen. I've tried him, and he says this girl is a natural hoodlum, and mentally and physically healthy. He says she's got more intelligence than any ten girls in Vassar. She *must* be smart, too, because she told him he was a fool, and I agree with her."

Dr. Burt was silent, for he was intensely ethical and would not criticize a fellow doctor.

"I've heard a lot about you," the chief of police continued. "You're regarded as the best psychiatrist and neurologist in San Francisco. So don't talk to me about Doc Blethen. I want you to look this girl over."

His huge face brightened as he summoned a thought that would bolster up his plea. "She don't cuss me, doc. I've asked her all about herself, and I'm sure she tells me all she knows, but she don't know anything. She's bound to like you, doc, and when she likes anybody— Now, doc, I've got a notion you can get her confidence to such an extent you can prong down into her soul and locate the trouble. I hear men like you do things like that, nowadays."

Dr. Burt smiled. "Sometimes we uncover complexes or mental reflexes; frequently we do not. And when we have uncovered them we cannot always cure them. You say this girl has a ruined nose? Does it affect her appearance greatly?"

"She's ugly when you look at her the first time, doc, but after you've talked with her and looked at her some more the shock sort of wears off. I got a notion that if her nose could be straightened up she'd be a good-looking girl. And maybe if her mind could be straightened, she'd be a good girl."

"Know anything about her antecedents, her background?"

"I don't know and I can't find out. She won't tell me."

"It may be," Dr. Burt suggested, "that she doesn't know. Has Blethen finished with the case?"

"Yes, sir. He told me not to bother him about her no more."

Dr. Burt indicated his telephone. "Call him up, chief, and ask him if he has any objection to having me give her an unofficial examination."

McNamara did so. Following a brief conversation, he turned the telephone over to Stephen.

Stephen took the telephone. "Dr. Blethen? Burt speaking. The chief came to my office about that girl he has at the Central Station. He tells me you have examined her and gives me to understand she's quite hopeless. Notwithstanding your report he has asked me, as a personal favor to him, to see the girl. You understand, however—"

"Yes, I understand. Burt, she's a bad lot."

"Something the chief said has mildly aroused my curiosity. If you would care to invite me to discuss her case—understand I have no desire to intrude—"

"I'm through with her, Burt. Help yourself, old man. No question of professional ethics involved on these criminal cases and I can understand your scientific interest. However, take a tip from me and don't let that fellow McNamara sell himself to you. If you do he'll keep you busy. I doubt if any man on earth can run a criminal down as promptly as McNamara; he has a photographic brain and never forgets a face or a fact; but after he's landed a yegg in his cooler he develops an abnormal yearning to find out what made him act that way. Mac's a softy."

"Exactly. Thank you, Blethen. Still, a blind pig will sometimes find an acorn, and something he said— Good-by."

Lanny entered. "There's a young woman in the waiting-room," she announced. "She said to me: 'Where the hell's that bonehead of a chief gone?'" Lanny looked at Dan McNamara severely over the rims of her spectacles. "Friend of yours?" she queried witheringly.

"Yes," McNamara admitted, "and doc's new patient. Bring her in and he'll give her the once-over."

But Lanny shook her head. "This nut shop is closed

for the day," she told him. "Bring her around at one o'clock tomorrow. The doctor has fifteen minutes then."

"Lanny!" Stephen reproved her. Then to Dan McNamara: "Do you mean to tell me you left her out there unguarded? How would you explain her escape —if she had chosen to disappear?"

"I didn't think she'd duck, doc. She promised me she wouldn't. But even if she tried it, I got a plainclothes man on guard at the entrance to the building."

"But she might have gone out the back way."

Dan McNamara shook his head pityingly. "Them kind never have a coherent plan, doc. They follow the line o' least resistance, an' the front door's it in this case."

"Please bring the patient in, Lanny," Stephen pleaded. "And then you might—" He glanced eloquently at their empty glasses. Lanny glared at him, so he smiled—and she ceased to glare. But she went out mumbling.

Dan McNamara shook his head sagely. "Nothing wrong with that woman's thinking apparatus," he informed Stephen.

And then Lanny ushered the new patient in. She paused just inside the door, swept the room with a slow glance and permitted her gaze to come to rest on Stephen Burt, who rose and bowed to her. Instantly the frozen hostility in her glance faded and she smiled. "Reminds me of a gargoyle," Stephen reflected.

"Meet my friend, Dr. Stephen Burt, Nance," Dan

McNamara introduced her airily. "Doc, this is Nance
Belden, alias Dorothy Case, alias Fay Barham, alias
Elizabeth Vernon."

Stephen said politely that he was delighted to make
her acquaintance, and Nance replied with acrid directness, "Why?" Whereat Stephen Burt laughed and set
a chair for her. Nance plumped herself down in it with
a weary sigh, jerked off her jaunty hat and threw it on
Stephen's desk. "All right, Steve. Shoot! What's the
idea of the big convention? Another fishing expedi-
tion?"

"Now, Nance," Dan McNamara soothed her, "you
cut that out. You're not talking to Doc Blethen. Doc
Burt's a gentleman."

Nance remembered her manners. "My error," she
apologized.

From the doorway leading into the waiting-room,
Lanny gazed upon the girl with frank disapproval. Over-
Nance's shoulder she caught Stephen's eye and shook
her head sorrowfully.

"The old girl's shocked!" Nance laughed softly without looking around, while Lanny disappeared.

"How do you know, Miss Belden?" Stephen in-
quired.

"Mirror," and Nance Belden pointed.

"Close your eyes," Stephen commanded, "and describe this room to me."

"All right. There are two empty highball glasses on
the telephone stand back of you." She sniffed. "Bourbon. The stand's three feet high, and the telephone book

is in the compartment under the top of the stand. The
telephone is one of those combination receiver-mouth-
piece things like they use in English stage scenes, and
the telephone cord is white. The desk is solid walnut,
I think, flat-topped and clean. You have a bronze combination ink-well, pen-rack and pin-tray. There is a blue
crayon pencil and a red crayon pencil and a black, gold-
banded fountain pen on the pen rack. The fountain
pen has green ink in it. I know because on the calendar
pad on the desk, which is opened at November 23—
although this is the 24th—you've written something
with the pen very recently. You're sitting in a walnut
swivel chair, brown leather upholstered, and a high back
up to your shoulder tops. The chief's sitting in the rich
patients' chair and I'm sitting in the one the poor guys
use. The chief's chair is an overstuffed rocker, and if
you give him another drink he'll fall asleep in it. On
the wall back of you, there is a framed diploma in
Latin, issued to Stephen John Burt by Leland Stanford Junior University Medical School, and about four
feet from it is the Oath of Hippocrates in a black
frame, like the diploma. The print is old English and
done in black and red. Across the room, in back of the
chief, is a walnut book-case, built in detachable tiers,
and there's a white wash-stand in the corner close by
it. The rug is beige-colored and Chinese, and on the
wall in back of me, where you can look at it readily, is
a framed photograph of your father. It must be a
photograph of your father because he looks a great
deal like you. In back of me a door leads into the old

lady's den and"—here Nance opened her hand-bag, took out a small mirror held it up and opened her eyes an instant—"yes, I thought so. That door is ajar, and the old lady is listening to every word I say.

"Now I'll describe you. You're a darling. You're tall and you haven't started to grow a tummy yet. You're about thirty-two or three years old, your hair is dark brown and your eyes dark blue, and you have nice teeth, and they show when you smile. You have nice hands and your nails were manicured this morning, but you have a dirty spot on the finger-nail of your right index finger—no, it isn't dirt. It's iodin. Pardon! My error. Do I win first prize, doc?"

"In a walk, Miss Belden. You are absolutely the most amazing person I have ever examined. You are one in a million—one of those rare persons who not only see everything at a glance but take a mental photograph of it. And remember it. Yes, you win a prize."

"I'll have a highball with you boys," said Miss Belden composedly.

"You'll not, you little—this and that," Lanny countered from behind the door. "The very idea!"

"Then the party breaks up here and now," Miss Belden informed Stephen.

"Lanny," Stephen called, "I hope you aren't forgetting the laws of hospitality."

"Come on, kid," the girl entreated Lanny. "Buy me one and I'll get the chief to do something nice for you."

"What influence has the likes of you with the chief of police?" Lanny was emerging with two highballs.

"Do you drive a car, Miss Lanning?"

Nance Belden whistled sharply to Dan McNamara.

"Get out your card, Dan. Here's the fountain pen. Write as I dictate. Ready: 'To all Traffic Officers: The bearer, Miss Rebecca Lanning, has the freedom of the city. She has my authority to park where she pleases and she shall not be tagged. She cannot be arrested for anything except murder and even then she must not ride in the wagon. Signed: Dan McNamara, Chief of Police.' "

Dan McNamara obeyed, Nance Belden viséed the card, blotted it and handed it to Lanny. "Now, you tell 'em all who's kind to you, Rebecca. I'm some kid, am I not? You bet I'm some kid. Dan knows it and your boss knows it and if, by now, you don't know it, I hope Steve fires you."

"You are some kid. I admit it. Thank you, dear. You shall have a highball."

"Have one yourself," Nance suggested grandly. "Let's all be sociable, eh, Steve?"

"Miss Belden—" Stephen began.

"Call me Nance," the strange young creature interrupted. "Why all the formality?"

"Have you any objection, Nance, to telling me your real name?"

"None at all. I don't know my real name."

"Who were your parents?"

"I don't know."

"Why did you steal the silk stockings?"

Nance threw back her head and laughed. "Why, you silly, I had runs in every pair I owned."

"Poor dear!" Lanny was speaking. Her hand strayed over the girl's jet-black, shiny bob; her fingers sought a shell-like ear and tugged it gently.

Nance looked up at the nurse, surprise and friendliness shining in her eyes.

"Why, you're sweet, aren't you? Why, you darling!" And she lifted her face for Lanny to kiss. Lanny kissed her. Trust Lanny for that.

"It's too late to go further tonight, Dan," Lanny said. "Bring her in at nine tomorrow morning."

"Can't, Lanny." With a bound the excellent Mc-Namara had landed beside Lanny in the garden of friendship, as one might say. "She's due in the police court at nine o'clock for sentence. Right away she'll be waltzed over to the superior court to the judge that gave her a suspended sentence two years ago. She hasn't made good, so he'll sign the commitment papers, and it'll be some time before we see our Nancy again."

"Has she an attorney?"

"The public defender, that's all."

Lanny looked at Stephen. Stephen looked at Lanny. Both nodded. "Get the best in town, Dan," Lanny urged the chief. "Dr. Burt will appear in court and plead for a stay of sentence. We'll tell that judge a few things about criminal psychology and just why it would be frightful social injustice to put this girl in San Quentin."

She turned to Nance Belden, drew the girl's face down on her breast and patted the rouged cheek. "See you tomorrow, dearie," she promised. "Be a good girl now and be nice to Dan McNamara, because he's one of the best friends you'll ever have."

"Kiss me again, please," Nance whispered. And when Lanny had complied, the girl came around the desk to Stephen Burt. "I want you to kiss me, too," she said. "You're sweet—thank you a lot."

When Dan McNamara and his prisoner had departed, Lanny and Stephen looked at each other throughout a long silence, which Lanny was first to break.

"That girl's clean, Stevie. Not a touch of the slattern about her. She could pass the Binet intelligence test so fast she'd meet it on her way back. And she isn't tough at all. She's only trying to be, and she finds it uphill work."

"Defense mechanism largely," he said.

"Better go home, Lanny," he added. "Get a good night's sleep and try to forget what a sad world we live in."

"It'd be a damned sight sadder if you didn't live in it," she snapped.

Under stress of emotion, Lanny, as she grew older, occasionally indulged herself in a little mild profanity. Stephen didn't mind. He knew she was disillusioned, middle-aged in point of years, but old with the wisdom and sadness of the world, as only a doctor or a trained nurse can be; that she had earned her privileges. As a surgical nurse she had been sworn at by doctors whose nerves grew taut as piano wires, during a dangerous operation, and she had learned to give as good as she received—wherefore the men of her world respected her and liked her, for her courage and efficiency.

"See to it that you're on hand in court tomorrow morning, Stevie, with a sweet line of scientific argument to bewilder that judge and the district attorney," she charged a little later. "Good night, my dear boy."

Dear old Lanny! Once more had occurred to her the miracle of love. A stranger—a bit of flotsam and jetsam on the muddy sea of life—had looked behind her brusk, businesslike, belligerent exterior and found the great warm heart that yearned so for affection and understanding. Hers was a strange nature. She was so strong, and so possessed of the urge to share her strength with those she loved, particularly if they evinced any affection for her, that she was singularly democratic in her choice of beneficiary. Nance Belden, like Stephen Burt, had appealed to her thwarted mother love, and nothing that the girl had been, nothing she might ever be, would alter Lanny's opinion, formed on an instant's notice, that the girl was an angel. A dark angel, perchance, and like Lucifer, fallen from high place, but—an angel nevertheless.

CHAPTER FOUR

THE accompanying presence of Chief of Police
Daniel McNamara cleared a lane through the
corridor of the Hall of Justice, in which the police
courts of San Francisco are located, and enabled Dr.
Stephen Burt to observe how instinctively servile are
the human dregs one finds in such surroundings.

"Gangway there! Make way for the chief," a rat-
faced little man shouted, and then sought wistfully, in
the chief's rugged countenance, for some faint sign of
the mighty man's approval.

"So you're in Dutch again, eh?" McNamara greeted
the fellow without enthusiasm but without malice.
"Goin' to beat the case this time?"

The rat-faced man shrugged. "Here's hopin', chief,"
he replied, and tittered mirthlessly.

"Look at them," McNamara said to Stephen. "And
after you've looked at them, smell them! Nine out of
ten of them never had a chance, wouldn't know a chance
if they saw it—and if they did, wouldn't know what to
do with it. But what the uplifters don't know is that
these people don't really suffer. They haven't that much
capacity; their inclination is to make the best of everything, to be happy in proportion to their opportunities

40

for happiness. If they can't get happiness they put up with apathy. But they seldom know heart-break. That," he added, "is the privilege of folks with brains enough to have a sound appreciation of moral values."

He paused before a court-room door. "Nance is in there," he told Stephen. "I'll not go in with you. I'd have a week of rotten publicity in all the papers if I appeared to have any special interest in the case. Her lawyer's name is Tyrrell, and he'll call you as an expert witness."

Stephen elbowed his way into the court-room. Nance Belden saw him, and from behind the bars of the prisoner's dock waved to him and called cheerily: "Hello, Steve."

"Silence—you!" the bailiff warned her.

Nance made a face at him; then, observing Stephen lay finger to lip in a warning gesture, she tossed her head, tilted her chin and bent upon the judge a cold and defiant stare.

"Call the morning calendar," the judge ordered perfunctorily. The clerk of the court rose and in a sing-song cadence proceeded to call the first case. "People of the State of California versus Nance Belden, alias Fay Barham, alias Dorothy Case, alias Elizabeth Vernon, convicted of petit larceny and up for sentence."

The bailiff opened the door of the prisoners' dock and beckoned to Nance.

"Nance Belden," the judge queried, "have you anything to say as to why sentence should not be pronounced upon you?"

"I've got a mouthpiece," the girl retorted. "Ask him!"

From a chair beside the counsels' table a young man arose. "May it please the court, the public defender has withdrawn from this case and I am now counsel for the defendant. My name is David Tyrrell."

The judge nodded amiably. "Well, Mr. Tyrrell?"

"I am reliably informed, your honor, that, following a fair and impartial trial, this defendant has been convicted of the crime of which she stands accused and is now before the court for sentence."

"Any sentence I might impose upon your client, Mr. Tyrrell, will be quite a perfunctory proceeding, I assure you. Your client is now under a suspended sentence from the superior court, department number six, for the crime of grand theft. She was there sentenced to two years in San Quentin penitentiary, but paroled in the custody of the parole officer for two years, contingent upon her good behavior. Less than two months have passed since she was paroled, and today she stands before this court for sentence under a charge of petit larceny. It is not my intention to sentence her. The stolen goods have been recovered, and it appears to this court that no useful purpose can be served by imposing upon her a sentence of say ninety days in the county jail. The defendant evidently is incorrigible, and I intend to remand her to the superior court, department number six, for commitment under the old charge of grand theft."

"I thank your honor. I have been retained in this apparently hopeless case for the purpose of adducing a sound reason why this defendant should be neither sentenced under the present charge nor remanded to the superior court for commitment under sentence for the former crime. To that end, you honor, I ask leave to present an expert witness to testify to the mental irresponsibility of my client. If such mental irresponsibility can be demonstrated to your honor's satisfaction—"

"One moment, please, Mr. Tyrrell. Your action would be merely wasting your time and that of the court. I shall remand the prisoner immediately to the superior court, with a request to the judge thereof that her case be taken up immediately, in order to afford your expert witness, whose time, doubtless, is very valuable, an opportunity to present his views where they will do the most good. I sentence this prisoner to ninety days in the county jail, but the sentence will be suspended during her good behavior for one year from date. A bailiff will conduct you, your expert witness and the defendant at once to department number six of the superior court, and I will immediately telephone to the judge and request that he listen to your expert witness." He bobbed his august head toward the clerk. "Next case?"

Fortunately, as they entered department six of the superior court, the judge had recently granted a continuance in the case he was trying.

He glanced at a document which evidently had reached him from the police magistrate's court. "Well, Mr. Tyrrell, I am cognizant of the existing conditions with respect to your client. I understand you desire to present some expert testimony in an effort to prove the mental irresponsibility of this defendant, Nance Belden. I may state that I have already been in telephonic communication with Dr. Blethen, the neurologist and psychiatrist, who does the medico-legal work for the district attorney's office, and have had a complete report from him on this case. You may proceed, however, to present your side of it. Who is your witness?"

"Dr. Stephen Burt, your honor"—and Tyrrell indicated Stephen. "I think I do not flatter Dr. Burt when I state that he is regarded—"

"I know all about Dr. Burt," the judge interrupted pleasantly. "I had him in my court a year ago as an expert witness in the matter of the Carter will case." He nodded to Stephen. "It will not be necessary to have you sworn, doctor. I didn't swear Dr. Blethen. This court is very much interested in getting at the facts in this case, and it is obliged to you for your voluntary attendance. What is your professional opinion of this girl's mentality?"

"I have not had a fair opportunity to study her, your honor," Stephen replied, "hence I am not in a position to give the court more than a snap decision in her case."

"How long have you studied her?"

"About thirty minutes, your honor."

"H'm-m-m! Dr. Blethen examined her on three different occasions, his examinations embodying a total of about six hours' time."

"With all due deference to my distinguished colleague," Stephen replied with his singularly charming smile, "six hours is not usually considered more than sufficient time to form an approximate opinion, which subsequent investigations may set at variance. However, there are some cases which present such aspects that almost any skilled psychiatrist should not fail to be impressed by them, and form promptly a definite theory upon which to work to effect a cure. If this girl were to become a patient of mine today, I should devote many weeks to an effort to demonstrate that my original opinion regarding her was in error."

"Is she crazy, Dr. Burt?"

"Not in the sense that we customarily employ the term, your honor. I should say, rather, that her psychology is abnormal, that she is neither moral nor immoral, but unmoral. For instance, when I asked her why she stole silk stockings, for which offense she has recently been convicted, she told me quite frankly that she did it because there were runs in all her old stockings. That reply was very illuminating. As I talked further with her I noted her variant moods and quickly came to the conclusion that she is suffering from dissociation by reason of shock. In other words, this girl, who doubtless in happier days possessed a single personality and that a normal one, has now acquired a secondary personality. In plain English, two entirely different people inhabit the one body.

"The first personality, which I shall call A, is the result of acquired instincts, habit, education, and repressions imposed on society by convention and the code of procedure which we call morals. This has been submerged wholly or in part by a second personality, which I shall call B, and when B personality rules her she has amnesia for what I have termed her acquired or normal instincts. Out of her unconscious mind then emerge, as definite impulses to action, the old antipathies to such action, which we medical men term conflicts. Let me illustrate. We will assume that at this moment she is possessed of her personality A, and in this state she realizes she has runs in all her stockings—that she must have new stockings. She also realizes that she has no money with which to purchase new stockings, but she sees some stockings which she can readily steal. Normal people often have impulses to steal, your honor, and Nance Belden has an impulse to steal the stockings she needs.

"But here a factor intervenes. She has been taught, from the day she manifested thought, that it is wrong to steal, and this moral lesson has impressed itself upon her conscious mind. With repetition, the thought, becoming a habit, dropped out of her conscious mind to become conserved in her unconscious mind. Conserved there, it became a definite part of her personality—her soul, if you will. Thereafter it was not necessary to

remind herself that it was wrong to steal. She *knew*
it was, without having to think about it at all, and this
unconscious knowledge was her protection in the fleet-
ing moment of temptation, aroused by her definite need
and the knowledge that, lacking money to buy the stockings, and faced with the absolute necessity for acquiring
stockings, the sole alternative was to steal them. She
got no further than that vague, conscious thought. Immediately the knowledge that it was immoral to steal—
that nothing could possibly excuse theft—rose out of
her unconscious mind and became a dominating conscious thought. Now, right there appeared the mental
phenomenon known among psychiatrists as a complex
or conflict. In all conflicts the stronger wins—and in
this particular mental conflict, the will not to steal won
instantly. It was an older habit of thought. It was an
acquired instinct, whereas the impulse to steal was not
a habit of thought, because she had never indulged in
theft! We say we do a thing on instinct, but really we
act after due, if incalculably brief, cogitation, based on
reason, which is the result of habituation to doing certain things.

"This defendant, your honor, is a healthy girl as far
as I can judge from outward appearances. But she is
what you often hear referred to as high-strung. And
she is so unusually intelligent that I readily realized
there must have been a very potent reason for the commission of such as unintelligent act as theft. So immediately I commenced to question her as to her family,
her past.

"She could tell me nothing. She is not at all sure that her name is Nance Belden, and I am satisfied that her inability to throw any light on her genesis was not born of a desire to withhold that information. I believe she has amnesia for a certain period of her life, and we know that such a condition is usually the result of a severe mental shock. In such cases the patient usually has an intense desire to forget absolutely the unhappy, unpleasant or terrifying episode or person that produced the shock, and so intense is the power of will in certain highly sensitive people, women particularly, that not infrequently they succeed! Thus amnesia is produced. It is, in a sense, autohypnosis, and your honor undoubtedly is aware that people who have been hypnotized remember nothing of what occurs during the hypnotic state."

"I believe I follow you," the judge murmured.

"I have shown you why the normal Nance Belden would not steal. But now comes that mental shock I spoke of, with consequent amnesia for all of her life that has preceded it; or it may be a part of that life. With the amnesia comes what we term dissociation or mental disintegration. The unconscious overwhelms the conscious; the acquired instincts of morality—social usage—drop out of the conscious into the unconscious, and the thoughts and impulses that have lain dormant and defeated in the unconscious are now in the saddle. Unfortunates who have acquired dual personalities or a dissociated personality go from one personality into

the other and back again, with or without amnesia for
the preceding state.

"At a time when Nance Belden's second personality
(B) ruled her, and she decided to steal those stockings,
she was acting under the impulsion of an idea that could
not be combated. To steal had become an acquired instinct, or at least a very strong instinct. There may have
been a certain amount of repression against the act at
first, but gradually that repressive instinct, i.e., her
moral instincts, once part of her conscious mind but
now released to the unconscious mind, grew weaker,
until finally the stronger instinct won, and the result is,
we have Nance Belden up before your honor for commitment to San Quentin penitentiary on a suspended
sentence for grand theft."

"Have you any theory as to what this mental shock
might be, Dr. Burt?"

"I have a very definite theory as to what prepared
the ground, so to speak, for the mental shock, but I
have not the slightest idea of the nature of the shock."

"This is most interesting, Dr. Burt. Pray explain."

"Look carefully at this defendant, your honor. You
see a young woman about five feet, five inches high—
normal height for a woman of her age, which I imagine
to be about twenty-one or twenty-two. How much do
you weigh, Miss Belden?"

"A hundred and twenty-eight, Steve."

"A normal weight, your honor." He took the girl's
hand and counted her pulse. Then he took a stethoscope

from his pocket, placed it against her left breast and listened. "Her pulse and heart beat normally, your honor, and from her appearance of general good health we have no reason to suspect pulmonary trouble. Her skin is clear, soft, and smooth; it is free from blemishes —another indication of good health. Her hair is fine and lustrous; not dry and lifeless, as is the case of a person of pronounced psychopathic tendencies. Her eyes are full, lambent, kindly, intelligent. Her brow is full, broad, and of medium height, her head a little larger than that of the average woman, and she is broad between the ears—because, as she has brains, nature ordained that she should have room for them. She is neatly dressed and decidedly not a slattern. She gives no indication of dissipation—drugs or alcohol. But mark her nose. It is a grand wreck. A nose like that would cause a continuous mental conflict in any woman.

"But for this lamentable facial defect, this girl would be beautiful. Perhaps she remembers, or used to remember herself as beautiful or attractive; then this accident occurred and lo, she became an ugly duckling. She brooded upon her misfortune; she wept over it; doubtless she thought it very hard that God should afflict her so. Doubtless the knowledge that she was an object of curiosity or derision to strangers and repugnance to her friends made of her a gloomy, depressed recluse. Who knows what wild, desperate and desolate thoughts she became a prey to? Mental conflicts undoubtedly were at work—an impulse to run away, to hide herself,

countered by the natural impulse to make the best of
the situation, to be brave, to pretend she was not different. In the case of a girl whose mind and nerves had
been thus harassed over a long period, a new sorrow,
constituting a definite mental shock, even if of no great
magnitude, might nevertheless be sufficient to bring
about the condition of dissociation of personality which
I have described."

"Anything else, Dr. Burt?"

"I have given a concise and general outline of the
case as it presents itself to me, your honor. This
defendant should have treatment. It is quite possible to
cure her, and I am morally certain I could do so. Her
saddle nose can be repaired. I have a very good friend,
a specialist in plastic surgery, and I know he would be
willing to help, without charge, to make a swan of this
ugly duckling."

"And you think you could make her over into a
responsible moral citizen?"

"I think so, your honor."

"How would she support herself during the period
of treatment? By theft—or worse?" The judge glanced
at Nance Belden. "How do you support yourself, young
woman?"

"I carry my own checkbook," the girl replied.

"You have a private income?"

"Sure, old thing."

"What is its source?"

"I don't know. On the first of every month somebody puts some money in the bank for me and I check against it."

"And that's all you know about it, eh?"

"Sometimes I can remember, but I can't now. It's the times I can't remember that raise hell with me, judge. I don't know what name to sign to my checks then or I forget I have a checking account. Then I get hard up and steal."

"How truly remarkable, Miss Belden! Have you ever issued any checks that bounced back on you?"

"Say, are you trying to kid me, Whiskers?"

The judge ignored this obvious contempt of court. "I suppose you have had many sweethearts, Miss Belden?"

Nance Belden's scornful laughter filled the courtroom. "Oh, judge, you're precious. What sort of a man would pick me for a sweetheart, I ask you? Be yourself, judge. Now you tell one."

"Have you ever been married?"

"I don't think I've been married."

"Have you ever lived with any man as his common law wife?"

"Good lord! No!"

"Why not?" the judge pursued remorselessly. "Most girls in your social class do."

"Well, maybe because nobody ever asked me," the girl assured him with simple directness. "I don't mind admitting I'd like to have a nice sweetie if I could find one, but what the hell's the use trying? I'd only have him a little while; then he'd get ashamed of me and

leave me. What's the use bothering myself? I know a
blind fellow that's mad about me. I've often thought of
taking the poor gazabo on for my steady sweetie, but
he makes me so sad I know it wouldn't last. He has that
funny staring look, and when he walks with his arms
held straight out, it just breaks my heart."

"Where does he live?"

"God knows—now. I was taking care of him when
I got pinched. You see, judge, I took him to a doctor to
see if something couldn't be done for his poor eyes, and
the doctor said he could be cured, but it would be expensive. He'd have to go east to a very noted specialist,
who would charge a lot for the operation. Well, I paid
that doctor his bill and that left me short."

"Did the same doctor say anything to you about
your nose?"

"Yes, he said he could cure that himself, and to come
in when I was ready and he'd put me in a hospital and
operate. Gosh, it's some nose, isn't it, judge?"

"How did it happen?"

"I don't know."

"You don't know anything, do you?"

"Yes, I know something."

"What is it?"

"You haven't the slightest intention of agreeing with
Steve. That sheep-faced mutt, Blethen, has given you
an earful. You're one of these judges that believes what
he wants to believe. Steve's told you I'm nutty, but
Steve's wrong. I'm not. Steve's just a good fellow trying to give the little girl a hand."

"So you believe you're quite sane?"

"Of course I am. There's nothing wrong with me except a bad memory, and a beak like a monkey."

Stephen sighed and shook his head, seeing which, Nance crossed to his side, put her arm around his neck and laid her cheek against his. "Steve, darling, you'd be a wonderful sweetheart," she assured him, and laughed.

"Your honor," Stephen pleaded, "can't you see she's—"

"I can see she's as intelligent as you say she is, doctor. In fact, she's more than that. She is very artfully simulating mental irresponsibility by attempting to spoil the good work of her expert witness. It is my conviction that Dr. Blethen was right when he told me she was the smartest, most adroit criminal type he had ever examined. I believe, with him, that she is incorrigible, and incorrigible criminals should be set apart from society."

He turned to his clerk. "I believe the sentence was two years in San Quentin penitentiary. Verify it and prepare the commitment."

"Good God," Stephen Burt cried sharply, "you are not going to commit this social outrage, your honor?"

The judge eyed him sourly. "Dr. Burt, you will apologize to the court for that language or I shall fine you fifty dollars for contempt of court."

Stephen Burt drew a fifty-dollar bill from his pocketbook and tossed it on the table.

"Court is adjourned," his honor mumbled, much embarrassed.

The policeman who had brought Nance Belden into superior court approached her. "If you're a good girl, Nance, I'll not put the cuffs on you."

"You didn't put them on me coming here; so why should you think it necessary now?"

"You're an important prisoner now, Nance. The judge just gave you two years in San Quentin, didn't he?"

Nance Belden turned. "Did he, Steve?"

The doctor nodded miserably.

"And I'll not see you any more, Steve?"

"Of course you shall, Nance. I'll come to see you from time to time. I haven't finished with you—not by a long shot, my dear. Tyrrell, you're still retained on this case."

The lawyer waved his hand hopelessly. "We're licked," he stated, without emotion. "This is one hand no lawyer can beat, and I wouldn't try." And Tyrrell shook hands with Stephen and Nance Belden, put on his hat and strode out.

"Come, girlie," the policeman suggested.

"Well," the girl declared, with an effort at nonchalance, "this is a tough break for old lady Belden, isn't it?" She smiled upon him patronizingly. "You're a good scout, Steve. Thanks a lot for all you've done and tried to do. You meant well, but at that I think the old scientific hooey has got you a bit cuckoo, too. I stood for it a while because I thought His Nibs might fall for it, but when I saw you weren't going to get to first base with the big boob I called it no contest." She thrust out her little hand. "Well—good-by, Steve. I suppose I'm keeping you from other nuts."

She came close to him and looked up at him wistfully; so he stooped and kissed her. At once tears suffused her eyes. "You don't mind what I look like, do you, Dr. Burt? You're kind enough not to feel sorry for me."

Amazingly she had changed—slipped out of one personality into the other as one slips out of a coat. "Will you do something for me, doctor?" she continued, and he saw that she was all nerves now. "I'm looking for a girl named Penelope. I can't remember her last name, but I do wish you'd try to find her for me, even with so little to go on."

"Where does she live, Nance?"

"Out there, somewhere."

"You've been reading a poem, I think, Nance—a poem that runs:

"And you, my sweet Penelope, out there somewhere you
        wait for me,
With buds of roses in your hair and kisses on your
        mouth."

She trembled with eagerness. "Why, you know her, doctor. That's the Penelope I'm looking for."

"Oh, if that's the Penelope, why of course I'll find

her for you. Good-by, my poor dear girl, and remember to look for me at the gate the day you're released from San Quentin."

A deputy sheriff took Nance Belden to San Quentin and was decent enough to refrain from handcuffing her en route. The girl was not particularly sad. Indeed, she appeared to enjoy the brief trip across the bay in the ferry-boat, and the half-hour's journey by train to Greenbrae, where the prison bus meets arriving deputy sheriffs and their charges. Even the first glimpse of the penitentiary did not disturb her, for the road that enters the grounds is flanked by the homes of the officials and guards, and well-kept lawns and flower gardens give no hint of the gloom that lies in waiting beyond the main gate.

She was taken first to the warden's office, where the deputy sheriff presented her commitment papers; from here she was passed on to another office where she was measured by the Bertillon system, thumb-printed and photographed, after which a guard escorted her over to the women's wing of the prison.

The building in which female convicts are housed at San Quentin would readily be mistaken for a hospital, were it not for the bars at the windows and the high metal mesh fence that surrounds the grounds. Two young women were hoeing in the flower beds; along the cement walks other women strolled, singly or in pairs, chatting and enjoying the sunshine and the fresh salt breeze that blew in from the bay, less than fifty yards distant. About two hundred yards off the beach, some men in skiffs were fishing for striped bass, and with the exception of a guard in a kiosk at the entrance to the grounds, one would have to search in vain for the slightest hint of official surveillance.

"So this is San Quentin," Nance remarked gaily to her escort. "Not so bad, my boy, not so bad."

The guard did not answer. He knew that the realization of restriction rather than high walls constitutes the horror of prison life. He took her into a small lobby, where a pleasant-faced, middle-aged matron, in the costume of a nurse, without the cap, greeted the girl cordially and gave the guard a receipt for her.

"Come with me, Nance," she said, and led the girl into her office, where she took charge of Nance's suitcase, opened it and searched it thoroughly.

"You have nice clothes and toilet articles," she commented. "Have you more clothes at home? These will scarcely last you two years."

"Yes. May I send for them?" asked Nance eagerly.

"Of course you may. The women inmates of San Quentin are not required to wear a prison uniform, although we furnish one if necessary."

"Hurrah for our side," Nance replied cheerfully.

"You read and write, of course, Nance?"

"Do I look like a dumb-bell?"

"Well"—patiently—"here are the prison rules. Read them and familiarize yourself with them, and then obey them strictly. Failure to obey them will lead to disci-

plinary measures, and repeated infractions may lead to
solitary confinement. If you prove to be a good girl,
you'll receive credit for good behavior in the shape of
a reduction in the length of your sentence. Good conduct will also render you eligible for parole after you
have served half of your sentence; if you should get
into trouble, tell me about it first. I try to give my girls
a square deal, but very few of them try to give me one.
If you should think you're not being treated fairly, I'll
always be glad to discuss your grievances with you,
with a view to remedying the condition if I can. You
will meet some terrible women here and you will also
meet some who, had they been spared the unfortunate
circumstances which conduced to bring them here,
would be ladies. Conviction doesn't mean that a person
is devoid of all human attributes. You will keep your
person and your cell clean. You will not be locked in
your cell unless you misbehave. Your cell—it is really
a nice little room—will be sacred to you alone, and you
will have the freedom of the building and grounds. I
will assign you to a cell and show you up to it. Then
you can change your clothes and come down and join
the women in the recreation room yonder."

"You'll do," Nance declared, and held out her hand.

Her cell proved to be exactly what the matron had
said it was—a small, neat white room, with a neat little
white bed and wash-stand, and a small chest of drawers,
not unlike that of a room in a hospital, save for the
steel door with an orifice in the center of it, and con-

nected by a locking mechanism with all the doors in that tier of cells, so that the throwing of a lever locked them all simultaneously. Nance surveyed it with satisfaction. "This will do me nicely," she said. "Thank you ever so much, matron."

She unpacked her suitcase, stowed her few belongings in the chest of drawers, removed her hat and sat down on the bed to read the printed list of prison rules. But one of the rules interested her. She discovered she could write letters once a month and receive visitors once a month—if she behaved herself. "I must be mother's little lamb," she decided. "This is some joint to get out of, but where there's a will there's a way." And she set herself resolutely to discovering the way.

Before locking-up time she thought she had discovered it. It was the fishermen in the cove just off San Quentin Point who suggested it to her. In her stroll around the grounds she inspected the fence. It was sixteen feet high, of quarter-inch steel mesh, set on steel posts bedded in concrete, and it ran along a concrete base. A bare-footed woman, using her toes to cling to the mesh, could climb the fence readily enough, were it not for an eighteen-inch topping of barbed wire, strung in strands four inches apart and set inward at an angle of forty-five degrees. One could not possibly surmount that. Nor could one burrow under the concrete base in daylight, even were the means available, without being detected. Nor could one do it at night because then one was locked in the cell. But one could stroll down the main walk to the sentry box just outside the entrance and appraise the situation here. As Nance suspected, the gate was kept locked and the guard had the key; indeed, the gate was never opened except to admit a new prisoner or an official, or to provide an exit for a discharged prisoner or official. However, Nance did not despair, for the gate was narrow—two feet—and there was no topping on it. She decided she would climb over it some day when the guard's back was turned; ergo, the thing to do was to induce the guard to turn his back!

For a month Nance gave her thoughts over entirely to this problem.

CHAPTER FIVE

L ANNY came into Dr. Burt's office and laid a letter on his desk. It was dated from San Quentin, on the cheap prison stationery, and read:

Dear Miss Lanning:

I can receive visitors next Sunday. Won't you please come over and visit me? I'm so lonely, and you were so kind to me when I visited Dr. Burt's office. I have never forgotten you and never shall.

Sincerely,
NANCE BELDEN,
No. 43,231.

"Just think, Stevie," Lanny declared proudly. "She hasn't forgotten me, the poor dear."

"I suppose you'll go over."

"Indeed I shall. It would be terrible if I didn't. I'm probably the only human being in all this world the poor thing wants to see. You'll send her something, won't you, Stevie? I think that might please her."

"Of course. You might buy her some books and a box of candy."

"I think she'd appreciate a portable phonograph and a couple of dozen records. I understand model prisoners are permitted such luxuries."

Stephen smiled. "Well, I'll stand for that expense, too, Lanny. And I shall await with interest the report you will have to make on your return." Lanny beamed.

The following Sunday afternoon, therefore, Lanny appeared at the warden's office, secured permission to visit Nance Belden and was duly admitted to the women's enclosure. After scrutinizing her pass, the matron admitted her to the visitors' room and sent for Nance, who arrived on the run and cast herself joyously into Lanny's welcoming arms. Then Nance led her visitor into a corner, and speaking swiftly and in a low voice, said:

"We aren't permitted to be alone with our visitors, Lanny. You'll notice the matron remains in the room. She won't listen to what we have to say but she keeps her eyes on us. Will you smuggle a letter out for me? I've got one all written, but the matron reads all our letters before posting them—and I can't have her read this one. It's to a very dear friend and I just couldn't bear to have her read it. Besides, if she read it, she wouldn't mail it."

Lanny's face grew grave. "Do you realize, my dear, what you are asking me to do?"

"Certainly. I wouldn't ask anybody but you to do it, Lanny dear. You're so understanding. If you can smuggle the letter out for me it will mean that within a month I'll be out, too. I'm sorry I cannot give you all my confidence, Lanny, but I just can't. You're the only woman on earth I'd trust, the only woman who has ever been kind to me. And, oh, Lanny dear, I do appreciate your friendship so." And Nance commenced to weep, the big tears, cascading down past her "saddle" nose, lending to her face an atmosphere of poignant ridiculousness.

Lanny comforted the girl and considered her request. Considered it sympathetically, too, for at heart she was an outlaw herself. And she was human enough to possess the generally human instinct of dislike and distrust of all policemen and wardens. She knew Nance Belden did not belong here; that if the girl had had a fair chance, if she had not been the victim of a code of justice born of ignorance and lack of sympathy, she would be in a sanitarium instead. Her hesitation informed Nance Belden that Lanny was wavering, and with the adroitness of a woman she pressed her purpose home.

"You can read the letter when you get home, Lanny," she pleaded, "and if you do not approve of it, you need not mail it. That's fair, isn't it?"

Lanny fell into the trap. "Yes, that's fair," she agreed, for she had unbounded confidence in her own judgment of what was right and what was wrong.

"You old sweetheart," Nance breathed, and kissed her—and at that moment a tall, handsome brunette who had repaid her lover's faithlessness by killing him, and who had been standing around in the hall near the entrance to the visitors' room, moved off down the corridor toward the recreation room. At once a shrill scream penetrated the visitors' room; then another and another

—a woman cursed—another cried: "Stop them or they'll hurt each other."

The matron, realizing that a battle had started between her temperamental charges in the recreation room, immediately left the visitors' room to quell the disturbance. Instantly Nance Belden drew a thick envelope from her bosom, unlocked Lanny's hand-bag and thrust the envelope in. She beamed proudly upon Lanny.

"I staged that ruckus," she confessed. "We have to play the game with each other here, you know—and two lifers obliged me. Good behavior doesn't mean time off for them, you know—and a hair-pulling match isn't taken too seriously here. Oh, by the way, what's your address—I mean your home address and telephone number?"

"It's in the telephone book," Lanny replied, and wondered why Nance had requested the information.

"Kiss me again, you dear thing," Nance commanded.

Then she was out of the visitors' room, running for the scene of the excitement in the recreation room. She met the matron hurrying back to the visitors' room, after having quelled the fight by her mere appearance.

"You left me alone," Nance explained, "and that's against the rules. So I followed. I didn't want you to think I'd take advantage of you."

The matron smiled and pinched the girl's cheek. "You funny girl," she said. "You don't belong here and it's a shame you have to be here. You have a fine code of honor, Nance, even if they did hang it on you for shoplifting."

She nodded to Lanny as the latter passed out of the building. The guard at the entrance took up her pass, looked her over with a pretense of suspicion, opened the gate and let her through. Outside the main entrance to the prison she climbed into her little car and had just started it when a good-looking but somewhat flashy young woman came to the side of the car and said:

"Are you driving to Greenbrae, madam?"

Lanny nodded.

"I wonder if you'd give me a lift that far. The bus doesn't leave for an hour and I—"

"By all means," the generous Lanny agreed, and opened the door. The girl thanked her smilingly and climbed in. Half-way down to Greenbrae, her guest said: "I think one of your rear tires is flat, madam."

"I was beginning to think so, too. It's bumpy, isn't it? Oh, dear, I loathe changing a tire."

Lanny pulled up to the side of the road and got out, leaving her hand-bag beside her on the seat. Instantly her guest opened it, abstracted the letter Nance had given her and tucked it in her own hand-bag; then got out and with Lanny surveyed the flat rear tire.

"I'll help," she promised eagerly. "The least I can do to repay your hospitality."

Between them they shifted the wheels and resumed the journey. At Greenbrae the girl out and thanked Lanny, who continued on down to the ferry at Sausa-

lito; no sooner had her little car disappeared behind a
curve than the girl waved to a sedan parked back of
the little station and climbed in beside a young man
who sat behind the wheel.

"Well?" he queried, apparently without interest.

"It worked," she replied. "Let's go."

Arrived at the little bungalow she occupied in St.
Francis Wood, Lanny put her car in the garage, entered
her home, and sat down to read Nance Belden's letter.
And when she failed to find it she did some of the logi-
cal thinking of which she was so eminently capable in
situations where her emotions were not being preyed
upon.

"Good work," she decided finally. "That girl I
picked up on the road to Greenbrae stole it out of my
hand-bag when I got out to look at the flat tire. She
must have visited Nance before I got there. She was
a flashy sort of damsel, too, now that I think of it. An
underworld huzzy, doubtless; doubtless, too, known to
the police. So Nance had no opportunity to slip her the
letter. The matron watched too closely. Nance feared
that would be the case, so she had an alternative plan.
What a shrewd judge of human nature that girl is!
She knew she could work on me, and oh, what a fool I
was to permit it! Why, I'm as lawless as she is, only
I'm a responsible member of society and she isn't.
Nance knew I wouldn't fail to visit her; so she described me to her confederate, who spotted me when I
drove up to the main gate and parked my car. When

the confederate saw me coming back she drove a nail
about an inch into my rear tire—simple as two and two
are four. The nail was driven all the way in and the air
was out before we'd gone a mile. Oh, dear, dear, dear,
what a simpleton I am! I suppose I ought to do something about this, but then if I do, how can I explain
my conduct to the prison officials?"

She realized thoroughly now the extent to which she
had been an accessory before the act. What act? she
wondered. And, wondering, she flew into a fine rage,
which was all she could do about it. Well, she would
have to keep the details of this adventure to herself.
Even Stephen Burt could not share her confidence in
this, for Lanny was justly proud of her intelligence
and integrity and loathed the thought that a suspicion
of either might obtain in the mind of her beloved Stevie.
She feared, should he learn of her adventure, that he
would never quite trust her again. And that would be
unbearable.

That sly minx—telling her she could read the letter
before mailing it; that if she did not approve of its
contents she was free to destroy it. That was the point
upon which the susceptible Lanny had impaled herself.

"Well, it can't be anything so very important," she
decided finally. "It couldn't be part of a plan to escape,
because escape from that place is impossible. Besides,
no woman convict has ever succeeded in escaping from
San Quentin. In all probability it was just a private
message to one of her old underworld friends. That

girl is too intelligent to dream of formulating plans for escape. Why, she couldn't get out of the front gate. She'd have to swim the bay to escape, even if she succeeded in getting through the exit from the woman's quarters and past that suspicious guard in the little house there."

So Lanny made herself a highball and resolved to dismiss all thought of the incident. She also resolved to give Nance Belden a piece of her mind if and when she decided to visit her again. And she was not at all certain she would make Nance another visit.

Two weeks later, while she was sitting before the fire, reading, her telephone rang and a man's voice said:

"Is this Miss Rebecca Lanning?"

"Yes. Who is this?"

"Never mind. You wouldn't know me if I told you who I am. I'm a friend of Nance Belden's."

"Oh, indeed." Ironically. "And who might Nance Belden be?'

Lanny was nobody's fool. On the instant every sense was alert, for if this was a trap set by the authorities, who, in some mysterious way, had got wind of her escapade, she was resolved not to walk into it.

"Are you going to be at home for an hour, Miss Lanning?" the voice pursued. It was a pleasant enough voice, Lanny reflected.

"I am, but what business is that of yours?"

"Oh, well, if you're going to be such a cut-up," the voice rejoined, "I'll not bother to argue with you over the phone. I'll come out. Good-by."

He hung up, leaving Lanny in a state of acute mental perturbation, which did not subside until she heard her door-bell ringing some ten minutes later. It subsided then. Her courage always mounted when there was an immediate situation to face. "Nance Belden's friend," she decided instantly. "And God knows what he's up to. Murder and robbery, doubtless," she thought.

For a moment she considered telephoning Dan Mc-Namara, then decided the worthy fellow might prove an embarrassment. So she got a pistol from her bureau drawer—because she was a practical soul and dwelt alone, she had purchased that pistol as a precaution—and went to the door. She cocked the pistol, took a long breath, threw open the door suddenly and raised her weapon.

"Put 'em up," she commanded harshly.

"Don't be silly, Lanny dear," a soft voice entreated her wearily. "It's only me."

"Nancy Belden—you little devil," Lanny almost shouted. "Come in here this instant."

Nance Belden reeled in, and Lanny closed the door behind her, turned the bolt, switched on the hall light —and screamed.

"Pipe down," Nance commanded, in that queer, faint, weary voice. "I'm not a corpse, but I'll tell the world I came mighty close to being one just before lock-up time this afternoon. Lanny, dear, I crashed the gate."

"Well, you'll crash out of here in a split second, you

little hellion," Lanny cried sharply. "Wet as a dish-rag and your hair like a witch's, and covered with blood. Where are you hurt?"

"Bullet through my left arm, high up near the shoulder. That guard could shoot and he did! If my boy friend hadn't shot back at him and made him hunt his hole I'd be fish-bait this minute."

"You've got to get out of here, Nance." Lanny was terrified. "How many visitors have you had since you've been in San Quentin?"

"Just you, Lanny."

"The authorities will look me up and they'll come here. Understand? They'll come here—there, they're on the telephone now. Oh, my good lord, what have I done to deserve this?"

She dashed into her kitchen and took down the telephone receiver. And again a masculine voice said:

"Miss Rebecca Lanning?"

Lanny controlled herself. "Yes," she said calmly. "Who's speaking?"

"Dan McNamara."

"Oh, hello, Dan. How are you?"

"Fine, Lanny. How's yourself?"

"Well, I might be dead for all the interest you've taken in me since you swallowed that good highball you grafted off me the day you came to Dr. Burt's office with that Nance Belden girl." She added archly—"You egg!"

Dan McNamara laughed. "Can I come out now?"

"The very idea. Of course not. It's almost ten o'clock and I'm just about to retire!"

"This is business, Lanny. I've got to see you at once."

"I didn't know the police were after me."

"The police aren't, but the chief is. Lanny, that Nance Belden escaped from San Quentin late this afternoon. She got to San Francisco all right. We know that because we found the speed boat she crossed the bay in tied up in the yacht harbor at the Marina. There was blood all over the cockpit and bullet holes in the hull."

"All of which proves, Dan, that God's in His heaven and all's well with the world. Are you seriously trying to recover the girl and send her back to the penitentiary?"

"I'm not. I'd give two of my big buck teeth to see her make a clean getaway. You know that. But the warden has raised a hue and cry—naturally. It seems you visited Nance two weeks ago and smuggled a letter out for her and mailed it."

"Dan, I give you my word of honor I neither mailed a letter for her nor passed it to somebody else to mail. Nor did the girl discuss with me any plans for her escape. If she had I would have told the warden, in order to prevent her escape. It wouldn't have been kind not to do so. The girl is mentally irresponsible and it would have occurred to me that, in any mad attempt to escape, a guard might shoot at her."

"Well, a guard did, and he hit her, too. But he didn't stop her. Her outside gang opened on him with a

Tommy gun from a speed-boat off the point, and made him hunt his hole. Nance swam out to the boat under cover of their protective fire; they hauled her in and beat it forty-five miles an hour across San Pablo Bay and headed up toward Carquinez Straits, while daylight lasted. After dark they doused their lights and sneaked back. The warden telephoned Central Office here and gave the alarm. I wasn't on hand, but of course the captain on duty had the water-front covered at once. He had two men at the St. Francis Yacht Club and they saw a speed-boat sneak in and across the little harbor to a vacant berth on the Marina side. Before the cops could hurry across, the people in the boat jumped out and into a waiting car. The cops followed in a police car as soon as they could, but one of Nance's friends riddled their front tires with machine-gun bullets and the trail was lost."

"How exciting, Dan!"

"Yes, and it will be more exciting for you, Lanny. I got home about two minutes ago and my 'phone was ringing. It was Central Office trying to report to me. They're just starting a couple of dicks out in a cruiser to watch and see if Nance tries to make your house. You're a trained nurse. The warden's found out that much—matter of looking you up in the San Francisco directory. So he thinks that she'll head for your house to receive medical attention. She got hit, you know. And you must be a friend of hers—otherwise why did you call upon her?"

"Dan," said Lanny desperately, "she's here now!"

"Into your car with her, Lanny, and beat it out to my house with her." He gave her the address. "That's the last place on earth the devil himself would hunt for an escaped convict."

"I've just heard a thump and a crash in my living-room, Dan. I think she's fainted. Telephone Dr. Burt to come to your home—that he will have to probe a bullet wound and dress it. Tell him to bring some whisky and two or three hot-water bags, and be on hand yourself to let me in. I can't leave here until I've mopped up any blood-stains she may have left on the sidewalk and my front steps. Good-by."

Lanny was right. Nance Belden lay on the floor of the living-room in a faint. But Lanny, the practical, wasted no time administering first aid. That could wait. A faint never stampeded Lanny. She picked the girl up in her strong arms and carried her down a short flight of stairs that led from her kitchen to the garage below. She heaved her into the car, ran back upstairs, got a wet mop, and by the light of the electric lamp over the front entrance searched for drops of blood. She found a few and followed them to the sidewalk, eradicating them with vigorous sweeps of the mop, then dashed back into the house, jammed on her hat and coat, ran outside again, threw open the garage door and backed her car out. She paused again to shut it, then swung up the street just as the half-red lamps of a police cruising car turned the corner. She swung wide to give it a clear berth, turned the first corner and spurted.

She followed a zigzag course until she felt sure she had thrown the police car off her trail—provided they had become suspicious and started to follow her; she turned up a residence street that she felt reasonably certain would not be patrolled by traffic officers at that hour of the night, and speeded up.

Dan McNamara was standing on the sidewalk in front of his house when she drew up. He reached into her car, lifted Nance Belden out and ran with her down an alley alongside the house to the basement entrance, which he kicked open. Lanny followed. Up the stairs to the kitchen the big chief ran, through the kitchen and on to a rear bedroom. Lanny jerked a small rug off the floor, and threw it on the bed. "Let her bleed on that for a while," she commanded. No sense in messing this nice clean bed all up. There must be blood in my car, Dan. Take a wet towel and go out and clean it thoroughly, please, while I'm undressing this poor lamb. Get me one of your wife's clean night-gowns."

"Ain't got no wife, Lanny. Use one of mine."

"Just as good as any. Get it. Who takes care of you here?"

"My mother."

"Can she be trusted?"

"I've sent her to the country for a month," he evaded. "I'm sleeping here and eating down-town."

"God bless our home, Dan. Clear out—and watch for Stevie and let him in."

She ran to the kitchen, turned on the hot water and set an enameled skillet under the faucet; then returned and undressed the girl. In the bathroom she found clean towels and placed a cold one on her head. When she returned to the kitchen, the enameled skillet was sitting in the midst of a cloud of steam, so she knew it had been thoroughly disinfected; she filled it with warm water, carried it into the room and with a wet towel mopped the two holes in Nance's arm and examined the wound.

"Missed the bone," she decided. "Bled like a stuck pig, of course; piece of her dress probably carried into the wound. Where does Dan McNamara keep his disinfectant if any? In his mother's medicine closet, of course."

She found the old lady's room; there was a medicine closet in the bathroom, and in it Lanny discovered a small bottle of iodin. So she doused the wound with it, wrapped a cold towel around the girl's shoulder and tucked her into bed.

"Not so bad for old lady Lanning," she muttered aloud. In the living-room she found a brass box with cigarets in it, so she lit one and sat down beside Nance, with her capable fingers on the girl's pulse. Evidently the count was satisfactory, for Lanny scowled at the girl and growled: "You little devil! And 'I crashed the gate,' says she proudly. Well, if you aren't the little hell-bender! You've got the nerve of a lion-tamer!"

She found a comb and brush on Dan McNamara's bureau and combed and smoothed the dank, straggly black bob, and when that was done she unbent long enough to implant a kiss on the white brow. "Poor lamb!" she murmured. "Nobody's poor lost darling!"

The girl's eyelids flickered as Lanny ran her hands over the white body. She found it chilled, so again she had recourse to Mother McNamara's medicine closet, where she found a quart bottle of rubbing alcohol, with which she proceeded at once to give an invigorating rub. In the midst of it Nance opened her eyes, stared sightless for a while and sighed. Lanny continued the rubbing.

"Is that you, Lanny?" the girl murmured faintly.

"Yes, dearie. And you're all right, so don't worry. Nobody's going to take you back to San Quentin."

"The cops chased us at the boat landing, Lanny. Are you sure we shook them off?"

"Of course you did—the big boobs! Now, listen dearie. I'm going to tell you something, but don't let it disturb you. Take my word for it you're safe. Do you remember Dan McNamara, the chief of police?"

"Of course. Old Daniel's my boy friend."

"Well, you're in his bed. The cops were on your trail, dearie. They suspected you might come to my house, so Dan tipped me off they were coming and to beat it with you out to his house."

Terror shone in the girl's dark eyes. "I'd never trust a cop that far," she wailed. "Oh, Lanny, Lanny, you've let him make a sucker out of you." She began to weep hysterically.

"If you don't stop that," Lanny promised, "I'll bat

you over the head with this skillet," and she picked that homely utensil up and shook it at Nance. "Dan Mc-Namara's your friend."

"Yes, and chief of police, too. Lanny, I'll die if they take me back. They'll put me in the dungeon—I'm afraid of the dark."

"Shut up. You're not afraid of anything. You've got your little red badge of courage, you scaramouche! You afraid? My foot! Didn't you crash the gate and swim for that speed-boat under fire?"

"Machine-gun fire, at that," Dan McNamara supplemented, from the doorway. "They opened on her and the boat from the towers." He came to the side of the bed and grinned down at the terrified girl. "Don't you worry, Nance. You're safe. I'm a cop, but I'm not without some sporting blood—your getaway earns three rousing cheers from old Dan'l McNamara." His big hand strayed over her face. "Tut! Tut! You show the white feather now and back you go to the Big House. I can't stand a quitter."

Nance reached a hand weakly toward his and grasped it; she clung to it pathetically. "Sure, Dan. Cross your heart and hope to die!"

Dutifully Mr. McNamara crossed his abdomen and said he hoped to die; which appeared to satisfy the girl, for she smiled wanly up at him. "You're a good old hunk of cheese," she assured him.

She turned her head toward Lanny. "Am I going to die, Lanny?" she asked.

"Not unless I kill you—which I'm liable to do if you don't buck up and believe what I tell you. You've been shot, but it doesn't amount to much. You'll be all right in a week or two."

"Then I'll be good, Lanny." The tired eyes closed, and while Lanny stood by, wondering what to say next, Nance sank into a sleep of profound exhaustion.

"Let her alone until Stevie comes," Lanny suggested. "The wound has stopped bleeding. She's been bumped around so it didn't have a fair chance. Come out into the living-room and if you're as crooked a cop as you ought to be you've got liquor in the house and I've got to have a drink of it." Her middle-aged face was very serious.

"Those cops at your house will stick around, Lanny, and when you return they'll want to know where you've been. What are you going to tell them?"

"Tell them nothing. Let those two cops sit in their car in front of my house all night and watch it. What do I care? At least they'll keep burglars away. And when finally they do round me up and waltz me down to Central Station to be questioned, you'll do the questioning, will you not?"

"Lanny," said Dan McNamara, "if you were a man and on the force I'd make you a detective sergeant. You're a bear-cat, that's what you are. But you smuggled that letter out of San Quentin for Nance and turned it over to Sapphire Susie!"

"Indeed! Well, let me tell you, Dan McNamara, that

I'm a respectable woman and I never associate, if I know it, with ladies known to the police by such names."

"Maybe you didn't know it, but you gave Sapphire Susie a lift in your car from the main gate at San Quentin down to Greenbrae. The guard remembers seeing her hanging around the main gate, as if she was waiting for somebody; later she got into a Ford coupé with a middle-aged lady, who looked so respectable he took another look at the pass she had just surrendered to him and remembers that the name on the pass was yours. The pass entitled you to visit Nance Belden. Guards may not remember such incidents until something happens. Then they're fast on their feet, Lanny."

"And who, if you please, is Sapphire Susie?"

"She did a stretch at San Quentin for blackmail. She was discharged a week before you visited Nance, and before Susie left the Big House, Nance fixed it with her to lend a helping hand. Apparently Nance didn't want to confide the minute details of her plan of escape to Susie. Susie's a swell looker but a little bit dumb—she levied blackmail through the mail, understand, and signed her name, instead of hiring a smart shyster lawyer. So Nance decided to send her written instructions out by you, and Susie agreed to pick you up, pinch the letter and deliver it. Did she?" asked Mc-Namara.

"She did!" Lanny was mortified.

"How did Nance slip you the letter?"

Lanny told him of the pseudo-fight staged in the

recreation room to lure the matron on duty from the visitors' room.

"Great," murmured McNamara. "And like all great things, as simple as falling off a dock."

"Dan, I assure you I wasn't in any plot to effect a prison delivery. If I'd thought for an instant I was doing anything wrong—why, Nance told me to read her letter and if I disapproved of its contents, to destroy it. I didn't see any harm in that."

"You violated the rules of the prison and you could be punished for it by a term in that same prison."

"I'm a respectable woman—"

"That gets you nowhere. I was a respectable chief of police once—and now look at me. See the hole that sympathy and excessive understanding has dragged *me* into. If your part in this leaks out you can only be punished—and you can't be convicted unless you talk in your sleep. If my part in this should leak out I'll be punished and disgraced and thrown out of the best job I've ever had. However—" he raised his glass to her—"mud in your eye, Lanny."

"Happy days, Dan, you gorgeous softy."

The door-bell rang, Dan opened it and Dr. Burt stepped in. He paused in amazement at sight of Lanny, glass in hand; she motioned him with it down the hall. "First door at the end, Stevie. You'll find your patient there."

"That girl with the dissociated personality, Nance Belden, escaped from San Quentin late this afternoon,

chief," Stephen began, and handed Dan a news-
paper. "Although it's Sunday night, the Monday morning newspapers carry the story in a seven-column head.
Big story. First woman to escape from San Quentin,
which adds to the interest." He gazed severely upon
Lanny. "What are you doing here, Lanny?"

"Behaving myself, I trust." Lanny was frozen dignity personified. With the adroitness of her sex she
shifted the onus of the situation to him. "Why do you
ask?"

"Oh, don't get so shirty." They were accustomed to
having little tiffs like this; each enjoyed bullying the
other. Indeed, nothing pleased Lanny quite so much as
to have her dear Stevie demand explanations of her.
That proved that he was interested in her welfare and
afforded her an opportunity to chide him for it. On the
whole it was a delightful arrangement. Realizing she
had him on the run, so to speak, Lanny decided to be
decent.

"All hell to pay, Stevie dear, and no pitch hot. That
Belden girl is here with a bullet-hole in her shoulder;
she's suffering from shock and submersion and chill and
loss of blood and she's cold as a penguin's tail. I've
given her a stiff noggin of Dan's terrible booze and a
fortieth of a grain of strychnin and an alcohol rub.
She's sleeping. Did you bring those hot-water bottles?"

"Yes," he said humbly, indicating a bag he carried.
Lanny fell upon the bag, and retired to the kitchen to
fill the hot-water bottles and tuck them in alongside her

chilled patient. "Lucky if she doesn't develop pneumonia, Stevie."

Dr. Burt stood looking down at the sleeping Nance.
"Out of the warden's arms and straight into yours. You
guessed she'd call on Lanny, eh? Dan, you're an old
fox."

"No, doc, I'm not. A fox has brains."

"He's a lamb, Stevie, just a big ram lamb. Well, get
busy, get busy! Even if you are a specialist in mental
diseases, you learned how to cut and carve and dress
wounds once, didn't you? And if you must know what
I'm doing here, I'm here to help you!"

Said Dr. Burt without enthusiasm, "Oh, take a jump
in the bay!"

CHAPTER SIX

WHILE Lanny was assisting Dr. Burt in dressing Nance Belden's wound, Dan McNamara sat in his plain little living-room and read the story of her escape from San Quentin. It appeared that throughout all of Sunday afternoon two men, in a motorboat, had been anchored in the cove off Point San Quentin, apparently fishing for striped bass, which abound at this particular point on San Francisco Bay. Other boats were anchored there also—eight in all. The guard at the entrance to the women's quarters had observed them, but as they were a common sight, particularly on Sundays, he paid no attention to them, until, about four-thirty P.M., just before locking-up time, a guard in one of the lookout towers on the hill had telephoned him that a boat had approached quite close to the shore and should be warned off.

The guard had thereupon stepped out of his kiosk and around to the rear of it, which faced toward the beach, less than thirty feet distant. He had shouted at the men in the boat and warned them to be off, that they were not permitted to approach so close, that they were within the dead-line. To this the men replied that they couldn't help it; that their motor had gone dead and the tide had set them in; that they were trying to make repairs and would be off as soon as they could.

While the guard was in the rear of his station, engaged in this conversation, Nance Belden had approached the gate, kicked off her shoes and, digging her toes into the quarter-inch wire mesh of the sixteen-foot gate, had scrambled to the top with incredible rapidity. She was just climbing down the outside of the of the gate when the guard in the tower on the hill saw her and immediately telephoned to the guard at the main gate; also to the guard arguing with the men in the motorboat. Upon hearing the telephone bell ringing in his station, that guard had walked back into it; at the same time, keeping the kiosk between her and the approaching guard, Nance Belden had dashed down to the beach and commenced swimming rapidly toward the motorboat, the motor of which instantly started, and the boat commenced edging in to pick her up.

When the guard in the kiosk, apprised of what was taking place, ran out with a rifle in his hand and shouted to Nance Belden to come back or he would shoot her, a machine-gun in the motorboat promptly came into action against him. He had not been hit, but a shower of bullets had spattered the ground around and in front of him and another burst had gone over his head and through the sentry-box. The guard had fired once at the Belden woman and hit her, but immediately thereafter, fearful of being killed, he had thrown himself flat on the ground.

The guard in the watch-tower on the hill had then

brought his machine-gun into action. His first burst had been short, and drew answering fire from the machine-gunner in the boat. Although the range was four hundred yards, the first burst from the motorboat tore through the wooden watch-tower, which rather distracted the aim of the guard there; nevertheless, the latter stuck to his gun and continued to fire, spattering bullets around the swimming girl and into the boat.

The men in the boat did not hesitate, but came on through the hail of bullets; the escaping prisoner had in the meanwhile either sunk or dived; at any rate a widening tinge of red appeared on the water. She was down about thirty seconds, then her head emerged close to the boat, and she swam with one arm to the side of it; a man reached over and grasped her under both arms and jerked her into the boat, which instantly turned, put on full speed and raced away close past two other boats. Fearful of killing innocent people, the guard in the watch-tower held his fire until the escaping boat was in the clear; then he and the guard in another tower came into action again. But a target moving at a speed of forty-five miles an hour is not easily hit, even by machine-gunners trained on rapidly moving targets; the fire was either over or short and the boat did not stop. When it was out of range, it turned, and in the rapidly fading light of the winter day, headed up into San Pablo Bay, running close to the south shore to avoid the chop of the waves in this shallow expanse of water. It ran without lights.

While the course they had taken would seem to indicate a desire to run up Carquinez Straits to the Sacramento or San Joaquin rivers, land, and escape in a waiting automobile into central California, the warden realized that his quarry was not lacking in intelligence; that, fast as they fled, they would realize that the telephone is faster; that the roar of their motor must betray them a mile away. He had, therefore, taken the precaution to notify the chiefs of police of Pittsburg, Martinez, Sausalito, Richmond, Berkeley, Oakland, and San Francisco, leaving to these the task of notifying intermediate points. The warden had a suspicion the fugitives would double back to San Francisco—particularly since the girl was wounded and must be hidden in order to receive medical attention.

"And here she is," Dan McNamara muttered. "Cripes, what a woman! Lord, how I love a woman with brains and courage. Just a little simple matter of taking pains and taking risks. She didn't go in to the dining-hall for dinner with the other prisoners. Smart! Knew she couldn't make a fast swim on a full stomach. Smart enough to notice the warden's oversight in failing to fill in with barbed-wire topping that eighteen-inch space at the top of his gate. Of course they figured they needn't bother with that, because no woman could climb a sixteen-foot wire-mesh fence anyhow, and if she did she'd only drop down into the waiting arms of the guard, who is never absent, night or day. But Nance Belden knew she could climb that fence barefoot; she knew she had thirty seconds to do it and a drop on the other side from the top of the gate. Her job was to induce the guard to turn his back—and her friends in the boat did that!

"She knew she'd been seen from the watch-tower on the hill and the guard at the gates notified by telephone; as he returned from the edge of the beach, around the south side of his kiosk, Nance slipped by him on the north side and was in the water as the guard took up the phone. Smart! She knew no guard will stick under machine-gun fire at fifty yards, merely to stop a woman convict escaping from prison. Smart! Sank and swam under water—and then the zigzag course between the boats of the other fishermen, after they picked her up. Fine psychology—she engineered it all—and I know she's a nut! And then straight to Lanny for medical attention—straight to the one human being she *knew* she could trust—no, I'll not send her back. And I don't particularly want to catch her friends either. I'll say they're friends! Wish I had a couple of friends that'd come on through machine-gun fire for me! I had thought the world was selfish and cruel and thieving and lying—but there's nobility left in it after all."

Stephen Burt came out of the bedroom and sat down and stared at the chief of police with grave interest. "Well, my good Javert," he said presently.

"Your good what?"

"I called you Javert. Don't you know who Javert was?"

Dan McNamara shook his head. "I never picked him up, doc."

"You wouldn't. He was a character in 'Les Miserables,' a novel by Victor Hugo. He was a fly-cop in Paris, and he pursued an ex-convict named Jean Valjean for twenty years, because he believed the man was a crook. Once a crook, always a crook, was Javert's philosophy. And when he discovered at last he had the goods on Jean Valjean and it was his duty to arrest him, he discovered simultaneously that Jean Valjean was also a good and noble man, which proved extremely embarrassing to Javert."

"I understand how that could be, all right, doc. What did Javert do then?"

"He climbed upon the railing of a bridge over the Seine, unpinned his shield, threw it into the river and jumped in after it."

"He committed suicide in order to give his man the breaks."

"Exactly."

"Well," Dan McNamara decided after pondering this a half-minute, "I wouldn't be boob enough to do that. He should have made a stool pigeon out of Jean Valjean and maybe he'd have gotten somewhere in his job."

Stephen smiled. He liked this heavy man, with the Celtic face as inscrutable as a Chinaman's. As a specialist in mental diseases he knew the part heredity plays in the formation of character, and one did not have to look at the chief twice to know that he came of courageous ancestry. No vague fears or anxieties in this fellow, Stephen thought. Courageous men are usually honest men; even when they are not honest they are sufficiently courageous to pay the price, no matter how high, for the things they do with their eyes open—to pay it cheerfully and refrain thereafter from whimpering.

"So you're going to protect this girl, are you, chief?"

"Yeah!" A throaty growl. "Got to, doc. Got to protect society." Stephen looked puzzled, so the chief continued. "If I let that girl graduate from San Quentin, she'll come out with a broader knowledge of crime and trickery and a greater contempt for society than when she went in. The only kind of criminal I fear is the smart one; I can always catch the boobs promptly, but sometimes it takes a long time to get acquainted with the artistic genius of a real craftsman. They're like writers, doc. They have a style all their own and you've got to learn their style. And about the time you think you've learned it, you pick up some bird that's guilty and he isn't the man you thought he was. He's just stolen his master's stuff. Nance Belden is too brilliant to turn loose on the world, doc. She's a leader—a leader of men. She'd make the balls, and her crew would fire them and always be covered up."

He ruffled his pompadour. "Well, doc, I've gotten her away from her gang. She's lost them and they've lost her. And they must never get her back."

"Would you like to know who they are?"

"Of course. I'm normally curious."

"I can find out for you," said Stephen.

"How?" Dan McNamara looked doubtful.

"Nance will tell me."

"You're crazy, doc. You don't know the code. They die but they don't squeal. There is honor in their dishonor, and in their weakness there is a strength that amazes me."

"She wouldn't do it voluntarily, of course, but just now, in her weakened state, I'm sure I could hypnotize her. Once I secure control of her subconscious mind, she'll answer my questions. And after I wake her up she'll have complete amnesia for the experience; she will never know she peached on her pals."

The chief smiled. "Of course I know that hypnotism is being used by psychiatrists. I've read some of their books. The modern chief of police isn't modern, doc, if he isn't a pretty good lay psychologist and psychiatrist. I don't know what a criminologist is, but I suppose he's a bird that studies the criminal actions and tendencies of criminals and tries to reduce crime to its lowest common divisor. That's the bunk. The thing to do is to know their minds and *why* they act like they do; if you can cure what makes them go, criminology becomes a dead science.

"Yes, I know all about hypnotism and I know something you've forgotten. Your power of suggestion on a patient in the hypnotic state isn't powerful enough to make him steal or commit murder if he's an honest man. His acquired instincts of morality, which lie in his subconscious mind, are too strong for you. And the most powerful acquired instinct in the mind of a crook is that he mustn't squeal. That's his idea of immorality! You try it on Nance Belden and she'll tell you almost anything but who her friends are, where they live and how they make a living."

"Well, we shall see—at another time. Meanwhile, what are you going to do with this girl? You can't keep her here, because that's dangerous unless you have her watched. And whom can you trust to watch her?"

"How about Lanny?"

"Lanny is my office nurse and I cannot get along without her. She's under suspicion now and we've got to kill that. She'll be watched, will she not?"

"I suppose so. Even if I pass the word to lay off her, I can never be sure one of my men won't watch her independently. On a case where it would be a big feather in his cap and mean a lot of publicity to capture a celebrated criminal, lots of dicks prefer to work alone and in secret."

"Then Lanny must not come to your house again. And yet this girl must be parked somewhere until her wound heals. She's suffering from the shock of this emotional experience now; she's lost considerable blood and suffered some pain, and for five hours she's suffered from exposure. Her garments are soaking wet."

"If she forgot to tell those men to bring some dry clothing for her to hop into, once she got aboard the boat, my heart will just about break. That would be one flaw in a perfect job—and I can't stand flaws."

And Dan McNamara strode into the room where Nance lay with her hand in Lanny's. "Why didn't you tell your friends to bring you some dry clothes?" he demanded. "Didn't you know you were going to get wet swimming out to their boat?"

Nance smiled up at Lanny. "He thinks I'm a nut after all, Lanny. Why, of course I wouldn't overlook that detail. I changed my clothes, but when we crossed the bay it was rough and there was a police boat on our trail. We had to outrun them—and you do forty miles an hour through a mile of tide-rips and you'll all but drown in the spray!"

"Thank God for that," the chief murmured. "I'm proud of you and your friends, Nance. I hope neither of them was hit."

For the barest fraction of a second Nance hesitated, then answered: "No, they got through all right, but why they did is a mystery. The boat was riddled."

Dan McNamara came back into the living-room and on his heavy face was the faintest, most cryptic of grins.

"I'm going to get one or both of Nance's friends, doc," he exulted. "One of them was hit, and he'll have to have medical attention. Not that I want to land either one of them for this job, but because I want to give them the once-over. At that they might be somebody we're looking for."

"Did Nance tell you one of them had been hit?"

"No, but she hesitated half a second when she told me neither of them had been hit! She never hesitates ordinarily. Her coordination is lightning-fast—well, you get so, doc, that you know when they're lying. Go to the telephone, call up your home and ask your servant if you've had any telephone calls within the past hour."

Stephen obeyed and was informed that a man, who refused to leave his name, had called up three times and had left word he would call again; that he had seemed very anxious to know when the doctor would return.

"I knew it—I knew it." Dan McNamara's pride in his own perspicacity was almost juvenile. "I figured Nance would tell them to go to you. And I'll make another prophecy. They'll admit they are friends of hers and that she sent them there. She's told them you're her friend and that you'll not turn them up to me. A wounded crook is always up against it, doc, unless he knows a crooked doctor. The hospitals and ninety-nine and nine-tenths of the doctors will report to the police when they receive a call from a patient suffering from knife or gun-shot wounds. And in this case the radios have broadcast the warning all over the state. There's a reward of two hundred and fifty dollars out for Nance, too—standing state reward for recapturing an escaped convict.

"Come on, doc. I'll go to your home with you and pick these birds up. The two men will arrive there, the unwounded one standing by his wounded pal, and I'll bag two birds with the same stone."

"No, you shall not. I wouldn't turn those two men over to you for ten thousand dollars. They're too—"

"Yes, they have guts. They can be trusted on a particular job I want to put through. Word of honor, Steve, I'll not pinch them. I just want to talk with them."

"Come on," said Stephen.

A block from Stephen's home, Dan McNamara got out of the doctor's car. He had already received from Stephen Burt a description of the ground-floor plan of his house and the location of the room in which he received the few patients who sometimes came to him out of office hours. And Stephen had agreed to leave his latch-key under the mat at the front door.

The chief watched Stephen put up his car and enter his home. A light was shining in the entrance hall, and this light Stephen, in accordance with the chief's instructions, switched off.

In about five minutes the chief saw this light switched on and off twice. That meant the doctor had received another telephone message. Then the light was switched on and off ten times. That meant the patient would arrive in about ten minutes, so Dan McNamara hid himself in the deep shadow of a tradesmen's entrance at the side of a house across the street, and waited.

In ten minutes almost to the second, a car, with

drawn curtains, drove up to the house and two men got out. The chief could see that one of them had to have assistance, so the driver got out and helped the other man half drag, half carry, the wounded man up the steps. Stephen opened the door and the three men entered; immediately Dan McNamara ran across the street and up the front steps behind them, found the latch-key under the mat, opened the door and stepped inside, closing it noiselessly after him. He could hear voices in Stephen's reception-room, so he drew his pistol and stepped silently up to the entrance of it.

"Put 'em up, boys," he ordered cheerfully. He threw back his left lapel and revealed his blue and gold shield. "No necessity to argue in the smoke. This isn't a hanging matter."

He forced the two unwounded men to stand with their backs toward him while he ran his facile hands over their persons and relieved each of a pistol. He "broke" both guns and placed the cartridges in his pocket.

"I beg your pardon, doctor, for entering your house unannounced, but you left your front door unlatched and I couldn't resist. I had a notion these men might call upon you. Just a hunch because the warden tipped us off to watch the home of your office nurse, Miss Lanning. So, while watching the home of the servant I concluded to watch that of the master, also. Sit down, boys. Never mind us, doc. The man on the table needs all of your attention. Fix him up nicely and let him

lie there until I come back. He can't run away, and
if he tries, don't you let him. You other men come with
me down to the Central Office till I see if we have anything on you. I don't appear to have the honor of your
acquaintance, but we'll look the Rogues' Gallery over
and compare finger-prints. While there's life, there's
hope."

"You're all wet, chief," the driver of the car replied pertly.

"Perhaps—but not as wet as your friends." And
McNamara chuckled at his little joke. "You can't do
forty an hour through the tide-rips off Alcatraz Island
without throwing some spray. You got an open fire-
place in your house, doctor?"

Stephen saw that McNamara was pretending they
had not previously met. "Yes, chief. In the drawing-
room. It's all set."

"I want to warm these boys up and dry them out.
They did good work this afternoon and they deserve
good treatment. Drop that wounded man long enough
to dig up a couple of stiff jolts of spiritus frumenti
for my lads, will you, doc? I always warm a cold man
from the outside in and from the inside out."

"Thank you, chief," both men muttered.

The three retired to the drawing-room and the chief
tossed one of the men a box of matches. "Fire up," he
commanded. "Then draw yourself up to the blaze and
drink the grog the doctor will give you. Where's your
pal hit?"

"Top of the right shoulder, calf of the left leg and biceps of the left arm."

"So he's the chap that dragged Nance out of the water, eh? He was in the rear cockpit, but you were up front driving the boat. There are forty bullet holes in the rear of that boat." He sighed. "These machine-guns certainly spray things. You didn't drop your own machine-gun overboard, either. They're too valuable and hard to get. A Thompson, I suppose. A Tommy gun and a Tommy man! Visiting brethren—from Chicago, I suppose. That's why we haven't met before. Pardon me a minute while I look for the Tommy gun in your car. And if you want to die in a hurry just try beating it out the back way while I'm gone."

He returned in less than a minute with the one-man machine-gun in his hands.

"We've got Nance Belden where you dropped her," he announced, "so while you're lapping up that whisky, tell me all about it."

"So Nance told you where to look for us, eh?" The man who had handled the motorboat spoke with withering contempt and hatred. Instantly Dan McNamara cuffed him viciously on the side of the head.

"Apologize for that," he roared. "You're so damned crooked you think everybody else is, too."

The man mumbled an apology.

"No, Nance didn't tell me, you rat," McNamara went on, "and I didn't ask her because I knew she wouldn't tell. But I did think she'd tip you off to call on this doctor. You dropped her at the home of his office nurse; I put two and two together and decided to investigate—all by myself. And here we are. Got any idea why I came alone?"

"No."

"Because I wanted to save you from the consequences of the job you pulled off this afternoon. I'm in sympathy with that, and as far as I'm concerned Nance Belden isn't going back to San Quentin. And she isn't going back to your gang, either. Now, you play the game with me and I'll play it with you. Double-cross me and I'll hang something hard on you, and you and your friends won't be heard of in public for a long time."

"Nance had no right to be there," the man protested. "The poor kid's queer." He tapped his forehead. "But she framed a sweet getaway, if it would work, and we figured it might. So we thought we'd give the girl a hand. She's all right. I've got a blind brother that would have starved to death if it hadn't been for Nance Belden; as for the man the doctor's working over now, Nance took care of his wife while he was in stir. Helped her when she had a baby. Chief, that girl's a saint. The only trouble with her is that she's a devil, too. You never know how to figure her."

"You've figured her right. She's queer. And what's your wounded friend been doing since he got out of stir? What did he get in for?"

"He got in for bootlegging and he's been bodyguard for a boss bootlegger since he got out."

"H-m-m-m! And what's your specialty?"

"I don't know what line I'll take up, chief. I've only been out of the United States Army Disciplinary Barracks on Alcatraz Island a month. I was a soldier—and I poked an officer."

"Oh, you're the machine-gunner, eh? Learned to shoot in the army, I suppose?"

"If I hadn't I'd have killed that guard. I could have gotten him if I cared to, but instead I scared him with overs and shorts. Did I sweep the roof of that lookout tower?"

"You certainly did—and rattled the man at the Browning gun there. Well, you're quite a fellow! What does your friend, the chauffeur, do?"

"Delivers bootleg. He took a chance for a friend."

"You may go," said Dan McNamara to the chauffeur. "Take your car and beat it. But I'll remember you and if you pull any rough stuff in this city I'll land you out in the grass. On your way."

The man fled promptly, and Dan turned to the ex-soldier. "I've got Nance out at my house," he explained. "Dr. Burt has fixed her up and I'm not going to turn her in. Neither am I going to turn her out because she wouldn't be out two hours before she'd be picked up. That saddle nose of her is a dead give-away."

The man nodded lugubriously.

"We've got to find a quiet spot for your friend, too," the chief went on meditatively. "A man with three bullet-holes in him is in an embarrassing fix—when he's wanted. So we'll take him out to my house, too. That's the only safe place I can think of."

"How about me?"

"You've been a soldier, so I suppose you can carry out orders?"

"Yes, sir."

"Well, your orders are to come out to my house, too, and take care of your friends. The doctor will call every day and tell you what to do. And you'll have to do the cooking."

"I can do that, too. Not fancy, but they can eat it."

"All right, you've got a job and a holing-up place as well. I'll go home now and get my car and come back for you and your friend. Meanwhile don't you get cold feet and disappear. I want to talk to you some more. I want to find out all about Nance Belden, and you and your friend might be able to give me a line on her."

"I don't know anything about her, chief, except that her real name is Penelope Gatlin."

Dan McNamara clasped his corrugated brow in both hands and pondered. "Gatlin! Gatlin! Penelope Gatlin! Now, where have I run across that name in my business? I don't usually forget names, and I seem to remember I had a call once for somebody by that name or else somebody by that name called on me. It was a long time ago. I'll have to look that up—I wonder if there's anything in the files at headquarters."

It was midnight before Nance Belden's two friends

were installed with her in Dan McNamara's house. Lanny looked both men over carefully and confided to the chief that she wouldn't trust either one of them as far as she could throw a bear by its tail, to which Mr. McNamara replied that one of them couldn't raise any deviltry if he wanted to, while the other dared not. Moreover, this latter was the only practical nurse he could secure. A trained nurse might talk; on the other hand, this friend of Nance's had been educated to keep his mouth shut. "And a very great virtue," McNamara added. "His freedom is in my keeping and my honor is in his, so we have to trust each other."

"If I had my life to live over again, Dan," Lanny declared, "I'd be a devil. Good people don't get any kick out of life."

"Shut up," the chief growled. "You're talking treason. Besides, it's high time you got home."

"How about those two cops waiting for me?"

"Greet them kindly, ask them their business and invite them in to talk it over before they can tell you what it is. When they tell you, permit them to search your home and be cheerful about it."

The phone rang and Dan answered it. When he rejoined Lanny he was smiling broadly. "You're a bum mopper-up," he accused. "That was Flynn, one of the detective-sergeants on watch at your house. He found two drops of blood you overlooked, so he thinks you and Nance are in the house but refuse to answer the bell, and he wants permission to break in, in the name of the law. He says he can slide the latch on your front door-lock like nobody's business. I told him to wait another hour and then try it, but to be careful. We cops pull off a burglary when we have to, but we hate to get caught at it."

Lanny's independent and belligerent nature was instantly aroused. "If I couldn't give a snooper like that cards and spades, the four aces, big and little casino, and beat him to death on the sweeps, I'd kiss a cow," she declared. "Guess I'll go home and make those big boobs feel ashamed of themselves for disturbing a lady."

"Whatever you do, be nice to them," he warned earnestly. "If you get snooty with them, Lanny, they'll just waltz you down to Central Station and stow you away for the night—with the excuse that the chief wants to see you. And I've decided I don't know you. If I did I'd go home with you. But I'm in a jack-pot now and must trust in God and keep my powder dry."

He escorted Lanny out to her car and with a flashlight examined it very carefully again for signs of blood. He found two dried splotches and wiped them away before permitting her to depart.

As Lanny entered the driveway and paused in front of her garage, there were no detectives in sight, although there might have been had she deemed it the part of wisdom to glance carefully about her. She unlocked the garage door, climbed back in her car, drove in, stopped the motor and switched off the lights. Then she got out, closed and locked the garage door and turned on an electric light switch on the door-post to light her way upstairs to her kitchen.

Then she almost screamed. Two big fellows wearing soft hats were standing behind her car, gazing at her owlishly. Instantly Lanny switched off the light, got her little pistol out of her bag and switched the light on again.

"Now what do you two handsome devils want?" she demanded.

Like automatons, the pair threw back their lapels and disclosed their shields. "Cops or no cops," Lanny announced, "my garage is my castle, and you can't come into it uninvited without a search-warrant."

The two detectives looked at each other, and Lanny realized that they appreciated her very much indeed. "She's a lawyer," said one of them.

"Not a very good one, though," the other replied. "However, Pat, let her have her own way. A woman"—the outrageous fellow bowed low—"and particularly a young and beautiful woman—with a pistol—always makes me nervous. If you will be good enough to open your garage door, Miss Lanning, we will go out, come up your front stairs, ring the bell like gentlemen, and ask if we can't come in and have a little chat with you. Is that satisfactory?"

"Eminently so." Lanny was as polite as the speaker now. She felt for the bolt behind her, slid it back and kicked the door open without taking her eyes or her pistol off the pair. They went out, closed both doors after her and held them closed until she had shot the bolt home again. Then she went upstairs and let herself in just as her door-bell rang; so she switched on the lights, removed her hat and coat, went to the door and opened it. Instantly, two large hands thrust two cards at her; whereupon she was aware that she was about to entertain Detective-Sergeant P. Flynn and Detective-Sergeant A. Angelloti.

"Good evening, gentleman," Lanny hailed them cordially. "Come in and rest your big flat feet."

P. Flynn nodded wisely to A. Angelloti. "She resents us, Amadeo," said he.

"Oh, I hope not, Pat. Let us hope it is not us she resents but our honorable profession." The wretch bowed again. "Thank you, Miss Lanning." And both gentlemen entered.

Lanny led them down the hall to her tiny drawing-room. Angelloti, like a hound, followed close behind her, but Flynn was in no hurry. He swept the runner in the hall with a flash-light first, then followed his partner into the drawing-room, and sat down heavily on a divan.

"Is this to be a long interview?" Lanny asked cheerfully. P. Flynn shook his head. "A minute or two."

"Then I'll not bother giving you anything to drink."

"Well, it might take ten minutes at that," Flynn countered.

"At least that," Angelloti agreed. "Besides, Pat, she

works for a doctor and her stuff is probably good old prescription goods. I wouldn't be surprised, myself."

"We been hours out in the cold," Flynn added sadly.

Lanny went into the kitchen, procured the materials and mixed her guests each a highball. P. Flynn drank half of his at a gulp, set down his glass and said:

"Well, where's Nance Belden?"

"I see by the papers she escaped from San Quentin this afternoon."

"She came here," Flynn charged.

"Prove it," Lanny challenged tartly; whereupon Flynn went out into the entrance hall and returned, dragging the end of the hall runner in with him. He turned it over and revealed a large dark red spot. "Blood!" he announced.

Angelloti touched the spot. "Fresh blood!"

"Human blood," Flynn went on. "Quite a clot of it. She must have fainted after Miss Lanning let her in. Undoubtedly she lay several minutes in the hall bleeding while Miss Lanning was fixing a bed for her."

"We know she came here," Angelloti charged. "We found two spots of blood on the sidewalk."

"That settles it," Flynn declared with ponderous finality. "Miss Lanning, you have this female convict secreted in your house and I advise you to give her up and save yourself a lot of publicity. Come now, give her up," he wheedled, "and we'll just give it out that we caught her trying to get into your house during your absence. We'll protect you."

"Search my house," Lanny offered in a queer, choked voice. She loathed herself for having overlooked that large blood stain on her hall runner.

Flynn and Angelloti needed no second invitation. They searched the house thoroughly and returned to the little drawing-room to finish their drinks.

"You've taken her away," Flynn charged. "Where did you take her?"

"Out with it," Angelloti urged. "You're in a bad box, Miss Lanning, and you'd better come clean. You can't fool me an' Flynn."

"If you're such good detectives, go find her." Lanny was getting her courage back again. "She did come here, but I wasn't fool enough to receive her. She came in a car with two men and she did faint in my hallway and lie there for a little while. Of course she expected —why, I can't imagine—that I'd hide her and nurse her. But she's neither a friend nor a relative of mine; she met me once in Dr. Burt's office where I am employed and took a liking to me—in her funny way. She's a psycho-neurotic personality. She wrote me, asking me to call upon her, and I did—like a fool— because I felt sorry for her. She should be in a sanitarium, not a jail."

"Who brought her to Dr. Burt's office?"

"Chief McNamara."

Messrs. Flynn and Angelloti sat up. They glanced slowly at each other. "The old man's been up to his old tricks again," said Flynn. "What become of Nance Belden after you refused to receive her?"

"She left in the automobile." Lanny was careful not to state which automobile or whose.

"You're an accessory to her escape. It was your duty, as a citizen, to hold her here, telephone police headquarters and have her taken down to the Emergency Hospital for treatment. You can go to the pen for this."

"Get out of my house," Lanny commanded fiercely.

"Sure, but you come with us." Thus Angelloti.

"You can't arrest me without a warrant."

"I said before you ain't such a good lawyer. We can always pick up anybody that carries a gun without a permit. Into your hat and coat, Miss Lanning, and come with us."

"I'll telephone my lawyer and then go with you," said Lanny with dignity.

"Nothing doing," Flynn declared firmly.

"You two dare lay hands on me and I'll have you both broke, understand. Be careful. Call up Chief McNamara before you get fresh with me. The telephone is in the kitchen."

Flynn went into the kitchen, called up Dan McNamara and told him his tale of suspicion and circumstantial evidence, including certain admissions made by Miss Lanning. He was much subdued upon his return, and Lanny smiled. "We'll get you yet," he growled. "You must have a drag with the chief. He's pulled us off the case. Good night."

When they had gone, Lanny put out the hall light

and watched them from behind the door curtain. They crossed the street to their car, climbed in and settled down for an all-night vigil—at least so Lanny decided.

So she dragged the hall runner into the kitchen, scrubbed the bloody spot thoroughly and dried it over the gas stove, reviling herself the while for her failure to be the capable counter-detective she thought she was.

CHAPTER SEVEN

TO the surprise of the machine-gunner, Chief Dan McNamara did not ask him a single personal question—not even his name. Nor did he question him regarding his wounded friend. He and the chief partook of a breakfast which the Tommy man prepared, and discussed marksmanship, wounds, battles, and sudden death. As the chief was leaving, he gave the machine-gunner a list of the tradesmen who supplied his house, and told him to telephone his orders; when delivery was made, they were to be left on a table in the basement.

"And don't you answer the telephone and don't show yourself outside or near the windows," he warned.

The fellow nodded. "By the way, chief, what's going to become of that speed-boat? It belongs to Nance. She bought it for forty-five hundred dollars."

McNamara sat down and looked his amazement. "She paid forty-five hundred dollars for that boat—and yet she was doing time for pinching a dozen silk stockings? I don't like to ask you any questions you might be embarrassed to answer, boy, but today will be a total loss to me unless I find out where she keeps her bank-roll."

"That's Nance's business and I'd rather not discuss it. She sent the check out in the letter outlinin' her plan of escape."

"Who received the letter?"

"A friend who showed it to us—and we decided to help Nance out. We both owed her a debt we couldn't see no other way of payin'."

"But didn't you figure out the risks?"

"Sure—and discounted 'em. Machine-gun fire ain't no new thing to us. We figured them guards wasn't top-notch machine-gunners anyhow—that is, at long ranges. They never expect to have to do anything but close-range work; they know how to handle their guns, but they don't have their regular periods of target practice on the range, like a soldier does. In our boat, headed straight away from the fire at forty-five miles an hour, it would take an expert to get on us. And they wouldn't know for sure whether we were accomplices or not until Nance reached the boat and we started pullin' her in; then, of course, they'd let us have it. But their first bursts on the boat were just as liable to be overs and shorts, and we'd have the girl aboard before they could correct.

"There were eight other boats in the cove. Six of 'em was in our pay and they was strung along in a line, so close together that as we run down the line o' them the guards would hold their fire for fear o' riddlin' innocent parties.

"And we had another advantage. That speed-boat

throws a wide white bow wave, and the water for fifty feet behind her and twenty feet on each side is a smother of foam when she's doing her stuff—bullets couldn't throw up any water that could be seen from a distance in the big spray. When you're machine-gun- nin' a fast-movin' target, you got to see where your shots are droppin' if you're goin' to correct your range fast and accurately. Then we had another advantage. The guards are in a watch-tower on a hill or a high wall, and at the early ranges they'd be firin' down-hill. Even the work of an expert gunner, firin' at a down angle, goes off considerable. The cockpit was lined with steel, so after the boy friend got Nance aboard, they flopped and were safe. The only trouble was that the edge of one burst got Cates before he could flop. The front cockpit was steel-lined, too."

The man grinned sheepishly. "I wouldn't take that chance again, chief. Those gunners were better than we figured them."

"You're both men after my own heart. Well, take good care of your friends. I've got to be on the job till midnight tonight."

"How long you goin' to keep us here?"

"You can bet your sweet life it won't be very long. You're too dangerous to me."

In his official car, driven by a policeman-chauffeur, McNamara motored down to Central Station, where he immediately sent upstairs for Nance Belden's record and photographs and proceeded to San Quentin.

"Did that Belden girl who escaped yesterday leave anything in her cell? Letters, photographs?" he asked the warden.

"I've been in such a stew over her escape I haven't thought of investigating that angle," the warden confessed.

Ten minutes later McNamara was in the cell, looking over the clothing Nance Belden had left behind her. On a slip he found a small, cloth-covered metal tag, such as dry cleaners clamp on garments to identify them. This tag bore the initials "N. B." Inside and just below the collar of a worn tailored suit he found the silk tag which tailors sew into the garments they manufacture. This tag carried the name of "I. Abrahms, Ladies' Tailor, 314 San Fernando Avenue, San José."

He snipped this tag out of the coat and rummaged through a suitcase under the bed. It contained a deck of playing cards, some clothing which yielded no clues and a blank check of the Security Trust Company, of San José.

"Nothing of interest in the girl's abandoned effects," he reported to the warden. "By the way, I want to have a chin-chin with one of your prisoners—Benny the Beetle, Number 41,322."

"Will you do me a favor, Benny?" the chief asked him when he came in.

"Only one, Dan? I owe you three."

"We'll forget the other two and collect on one. Do

you know the good-conduct prisoner who works in the identification bureau?"

The Beetle nodded.

"Know anybody whose time is up shortly?"

"My cell-mate."

"If he could bring me word that the photographs, finger-prints and Bertillon measurements of Nance Belden—remember that name?—have mysteriously disappeared, I'd be inclined to be his friend if he got into a jam later on and it wasn't too serious."

"I'll do what I can for you, chief. I'll ask Bender. He's assistant to the file clerk."

"See him in the mess-hall at noon. And see somebody in the prison print-shop. They're probably running off placards to send to all the postmasters in the state. That's where they advertise for escaped prisoners—in postoffice lobbies. Can't let those placards with the half-tone photos and Bertillon measurements get out, you know. Good-by, Benny, and thanks a lot."

From San Quentin Dan McNamara motored down to San José and called upon I. Abrahms, Ladies' Tailor.

"Mr. Abrahms, have you ever made a tailored suit for a girl with a nose that something has smashed flat in the middle?"

"Sure I have," Abrahms replied. "You mean Miss Penelope Gatlin, don't you?"

Abrahms looked in his card-index cabinet, then opened a large book in which he kept his customers'

measurements recorded, together with a sample of the
cloth from which each order had been cut. Dan Mc-
Namara unhesitatingly placed his finger on one of
these samples. "That was the cloth."

"Sure, that was the suit I made for Miss Gatlin
two years ago."

"Did Miss Gatlin live in this city? If so, I'd like to
have her address."

Ten minutes later, McNamara was pressing the bell
at the door of the house in South Mariposa Street.

"Does Miss Gatlin live here?" he queried.

"Not any more. At one time she used to live here
with her mother, but she has disappeared; and about
two years ago her mother rented this house to the lady
I work for."

"Where is Mrs. Gatlin now?"

"We don't know."

"Thank you,"—and McNamara directed his driver
to go to the Security Trust Company, where he sent
his card in to the president. He was received promptly.

"Do you happen to have an account in the name of
Penelope Gatlin?"

"Both a trust account and a checking account, chief.
We had her father's account for years before he was
unfortunately killed in an automobile accident some
eight years ago. We had the account of his divorced
wife for quite a while, too, but she has closed that.
She has married again."

"Do you know where she lives at present?"

"I do not." He was interested. "But I remember her quite well—a very beautiful woman. Her first husband was a splendid chap—retail shoe dealer in this city, and very prosperous. He and his wife had a row and she divorced him and got the child. Gatlin was permitted by the court to have the child on two Sunday afternoons a month, and one day he took her to a ball game and they sat in the bleachers. A long hard ball flew into the bleachers and flattened the little girl's nose; Gatlin rushed the unconscious child to a hospital and his ex-wife came and took her home before anything but emergency treatment could be given. Mrs. Gatlin was a religious fanatic and Gatlin suspected she was going to try to cure that ruined nose by prayer—so he kidnaped the child, was caught, arrested, and did sixty days in the county jail.

"While he was in jail Mrs. Gatlin fled to Europe with the little girl, and Gatlin was desolated. Subsequently Gatlin sold out his business, made most of his estate liquid and established a trust with us in favor of himself and his daughter. He had made a settlement with Mrs. Gatlin. When his wife fled to Europe with the child, Gatlin ceased to deposit the monthly check to her credit, in the belief that she'd write to know why. She didn't, but in some other manner he located her, and started for Europe with the intention of stealing the little girl from her. On the way to the station, an automobile hit the taxi he was in and Gatlin was killed."

"Did he leave a will?"

"He did. His daughter was his sole beneficiary. We were the executors and probated it. There was the ten-thousand-dollar letter of credit he had purchased just before starting on his fatal trip, and half a dozen pieces of city realty, which have since increased enormously in value. We advertised for the heir but received no answer, so the estate was closed and we handle it now, as trustee."

"How do you know Mrs. Gatlin has married?"

"She had leased the house Gatlin gave her in the divorce settlement, and about two years ago, when the lease expired and the old tenants departed, she came down here to have the place renovated and secure a new tenant. It was only then that she heard of Gatlin's death. She came to this bank, with her husband, making inquiries about Gatlin's estate, and tried hard to get control of it, but she was out of luck. That's how we located the heir."

"What is her husband's name?"

"I can't remember now."

"What were the conditions of the trust?"

"The income was to be permitted to accumulate and be reinvested, and the child was to have two hundred and fifty dollars a month until her eighteenth birthday, when the total income from the trust was to be turned over to her. She can never touch the principal, however, although Gatlin did provide that she might have up to ten thousand dollars of it at any one time if, in the judgment of the trustee, the emergency requiring such withdrawal was deemed good and sufficient. Gatlin had faith that the real estate, if held long enough, would appreciate tremendously—and it has. The trust is now worth three-quarters of a million and the income is close to twenty thousand a year."

"You say Penelope Gatlin has a checking account also?"

"Yes. We deposit the income from the trust semi-annually, in her account."

"Has she ever asked for an emergency withdrawal of ten thousand dollars?"

"No."

"Is her checking account active?"

"Not very. The cashier was speaking to me about it less than two weeks ago. She draws checks sporadically. Her checking account has interested us considerably for the past two years, because her monthly statement and dead checks have all been returned by the post-office. With the exception of about a dozen checks made out to local merchants and probably in payment of her bills, Miss Gatlin's checks have all been in favor of one Ella Cates, of San Francisco. We traced the Cates woman down through the endorsements on the checks, but she stated she didn't know Miss Gatlin's address; that Miss Gatlin visited her occasionally, wrote out checks and asked her to cash them for her at the local grocery store or drug store. These people stated that Ella Cates never received the money at once, but that they collected the checks for her and then gave her the money. I don't like the looks of this, chief."

"I'll soon find out all about it," McNamara promised. "And I know where Penelope Gatlin is—only I'm not going to tell you now. Would you mind letting me look over her old bank statements and the dead checks?"

The banker readily granted him the privilege, and McNamara went through the checks carefully, noting those drawn in favor of Ella Cates. The last one drawn was in favor of a man named Hugh P. Taylor, for the sum of five thousand dollars, and deposited by him to the credit of his account in the Federal Trust Company of San Francisco.

"I have all the information I want, with this exception." He drew forth one of the rogues'-gallery photographs made at the Central Station by the police photographer. "Is that Penelope Gatlin?"

"That's the girl, chief. Is she in trouble with the police?"

Dan McNamara laughed. "Not at all. She's the sweetest little thing on earth. The only trouble she's been in is that she's been lost. Amnesia. Can't remember who she is or anything about her past life. Has several aliases she uses at will."

"How interesting—and how sad!"

"Neither interesting nor sad—to me. We handle lots of cases like this. They're curable. You'll be good enough to regard this interview as strictly confidential, of course. It would be very embarrassing for the girl if news of her unfortunate predicament should leak out, for of course, after her mind has been restored to its normal functions, she will have no memory of the period in which she has been lost. I know a doctor that will fix her up in jig time."

"And after he's done that," the banker suggested, "have a plastic surgeon fix up her nose. She used to be as lovely as a violet."

"Sorry about that nose," McNamara lied, "but I've had the best plastic surgeons in town examine it and there's no hope." He held out his hand. "Thanks for your courtesy. You've been a great help. Meanwhile, don't send out any more of those bank statements and dead checks. Mum's the word."

It was nearly four o'clock before Dan McNamara left San José, and before doing so he called his office in San Francisco. "I'll be back in two hours," he informed the assistant chief. "Took a run down here to visit my mother. Tell Flynn and Angelloti to report to me at my office at six-thirty."

With his police siren sounding at frequent intervals, he came up to town in an hour and a half, went directly to the city prison and looked over the blotter to see what strange fish his men had brought in during his absence.

He found a member of the oldest profession booked for soliciting, and ordered her sent to his office. When she arrived he locked the door and finger-printed her on the appropriate card, after which he lectured her on the error of her ways. Then he went upstairs to the identification bureau and asked the filing clerk to have pointed out to him the filing cabinets containing criminal records for the years 1914-15 and 1916.

He was searching for a face that was photographed on his remarkable memory, and at last he found it. It was that of a young woman, black-haired and with a "saddle" nose, but not quite so badly deformed as Nance Belden's, nor did the contour of the face resemble Nance Belden's. However, since the original of that photograph had, to the chief's knowledge, been dead six months, he decided it would do. He slipped this record into his breast pocket and went back to his office. Here he carefully removed the three photographs from the card to which they were pasted in a row across the top. Below the row of photographs appeared the typewritten criminal history of the subject and in appropriate spaces on the reverse of the card appeared the subject's finger-prints.

McNamara picked up the fresh card, upon the reverse of which he had finger-printed the lady of uneasy virtue. He placed this card in the typewriter of his secretary, who had gone for the day, and carefully filled it in with Nance Belden's criminal record. Then he pasted over the top of this record the three photographs of the dead woman he had taken from the old files, carefully burned all the evidence of the substitution and dropped the ashes in a cuspidor, went upstairs to the identification office and handed the record to the clerk, who replaced it in the files.

Promptly at six-thirty a knock sounded on his door, and to his hearty "Come," Messrs. P. Flynn and A. Angelloti entered.

"I sent for you two boys to tell you, in no uncertain terms, to lay off Miss Rebecca Lanning," the chief began. "However, I owe it to you to tell you why. Miss Lanning is a friend of mine of long standing, and I know she is a worthy and dependable woman and absolutely truthful. She isn't interested in this girl, Nance Belden. It happened this way. I regarded that girl as a nut, see—and I haven't any confidence in the bone that does our medico-legal work. So I took Nance up to see Dr. Stephen Burt, the best psychiatrist and neurologist in this state. Miss Lanning is his nurse. She was very kind to the girl—very understanding—and the Belden brat got stuck on her. She has an affection complex, understand."

Flynn and Angelloti had had to listen, many a time and oft, to Dan McNamara's dissertations on complexes in prisoners. They nodded languidly now.

"Apparently," the chief continued, "Nance hasn't any friends. The poor lonely kid remembered Miss Lanning, so she wrote and asked her to visit her in the pen. Out of the kindness of her heart, Miss Lanning did so—and now the warden swears she smuggled out of San Quentin a letter with her plan of escape.

Well, maybe she did, but if she did, Miss Lanning didn't know it.

"Now, when the Belden girl came to Miss Lanning's home she realized she couldn't harbor her. Within a minute after the girl entered Miss Lanning had me on the phone and told me the girl was there. 'I've just heard a thump out in the hall,' says she. 'I think the girl's fainted. Better let me put her to bed, chief, and have Dr. Burt come over to bandage her wound; then the ambulance can call for her in the morning.'

"I thought that was a good idea. When she came back Nance was just going out of the door. Miss Lanning tried to stop her, but her boy friends were still waiting, and grabbed her and beat it. The trouble was that Miss Lanning thought the girl was unconscious and forgot to close the door when she telephoned me; so Nance heard her and beat it. Now it's up to you two to find her."

"How long have you known Miss Lanning?"

"Quite a while," McNamara lied.

"Well, even if she is a friend of yours, chief, she's no clinging vine."

"Well, leave her alone from now on and don't waste your time watching her house. The Belden devil won't come back *there* again. Another thing. We have criminals loose in our midst who are more important than a poor nut of a girl that only swiped a mess of silk stockings, so don't get excited and waste much time. That will be all, boys."

Outside his office door they looked at each other meaningly.

"He's up to his old tricks, Amadeo."

"Always feeling sorry for the under dog, Pat. He makes me sick."

"I'll bet a month's salary he knows where the Belden girl is this minute."

"I'm not quitting such a hot scent, Pat."

"We'll just split that two-hundred-and-fifty-dollar reward—and see how the chief likes it. That old girl warned us to step softly or she'd have us broke, didn't she? Well, where does she get her drag with the old man?"

A. Angelloti jumped to the natural conclusion of his kind. "She's got something on him, I suppose."

"Sure she has. She knows he knows where she's hid the body."

"We've got to see the Belden girl's photograph and thumb-prints and Bertillon measurements. They're in the upper office."

They went up to the identification bureau, called for the record of Nance Belden and studied it for a couple of minutes.

"I'd recognize that dame now if she was burned to ashes." Thus Angelloti.

Flynn drew his partner into a corner. "The girl was wounded. We know that from the guard that shot her and we're sure of it after looking at the blood in that speed-boat."

"If she'd bled that much all by herself she'd never

have gotten ashore under her own power, Pat. I'm inclined to think one of the crew got hit too."

"There's hope for the dagoes yet, my boy. You're right. It stands to reason some doctor fixed them up. Now, then, what doctor?"

"Dr. Stephen Burt," Angelloti decided.

"It stands to reason that if this Dr. Burt dressed their wounds last night he'll call on his patients every day until they're out of danger. If we catch him at his dirty work there ought to be a little something in this on the side, Amadeo."

P. Flynn thought that a thousand each would be a very modest sum to charge Stephen Burt for their silence—very modest.

An hour later they pulled up in front of Stephen's house, and behind a coupé parked at the curb. Flynn, circling around it, noticed a red cross on the radiator. He swept the interior with his flash-light, until he located the plate with the license in it, and read the name of the owner thereon.

They circled the block and returned, to park at the lower end of the block. At a quarter past eight they saw Stephen come out, bag in hand, enter his coupé, and drive away. So they followed him and came, in time, to a house, into which they saw him enter, as they rolled slowly past.

"He had a latch-key. He didn't ring the bell. And no lights in the front o' the house," Angelloti cried excitedly. "Drive back, Pat, and I'll get the number.

"That house," Flynn informed him dramatically,

"is the habitat of his Royal Highness, Daniel Mc-Namara, Chief of Police of San Francisco. I always knew he was a fox, but I never suspected he was fool enough to hide an escaped convict in his own house."

Angelloti was excited, for he was an Italian and even more mercurial than his partner, but like all smart Italians he was not impulsive except when he was in a fight, or angry. "This pinch will keep overnight, Pat," he warned. "It will keep several nights, because some o' these birds ain't in condition to be moved. So we'll make no pinch tonight. This situation is ticklish an' requires calm an' mature deliberation."

"Maybe you're right at that, Amadeo. Well, we'll stick round awhile."

They stuck around half an hour before Dr. Burt came out, entered his car, and drove away. "Drop off an' watch the house," Flynn suggested to his partner, "an' I'll follow his Nibs. I'll be back later."

He trailed Stephen Burt to the latter's home and saw him pull up across the sidewalk, preparatory to opening the door of his garage. So Flynn rolled past, circled, and returned to Angelloti.

"After you an' the doc left, I went up to the corner drug store and phoned the chief's house, but nobody answered," Angelloti confided. "The gang's in there, all right."

"I'm as nervous as an old woman," Flynn confessed. "I wish I had a drink."

Angelloti was a resourceful fellow. "Let's call on

that Lanning woman, apologize for our rough work last night, an' maybe she'll slip us some o' that pre-war Bourbon again."

Flynn nodded, and they drove to Lanny's house. Lanny received them coldly. "Have you come to search my house again?" she demanded irritably.

No mule's face could possibly have been longer and sadder than P. Flynn's. "We didn't come to annoy you, Miss Lanning. The chief's give us the inside story. We just called to apologize for even suspectin' you."

"An officer," Angelloti explained, "has got to do a lot o' things he don't like to do in the discharge of his duty. The apology goes double, Miss Lanning."

"It's accepted." Then they shook hands. "How about a shot in the arm?" Lanny, the worldling, suggested, much mollified.

Angelloti shrugged expressively. "Well, seein' as how," P. Flynn murmured. So they had three drinks and spent a very pleasant evening with Lanny, and she was loath to see them depart.

CHAPTER EIGHT

NOW, Lanny was aware that Stephen had planned to visit his queer patients after dinner that night, and she was consumed with curiosity regarding them. So she telephoned—and Dan McNamara answered.

"I shouldn't ring you up this late and get you out of bed—"

"Not at all. Just got in this minute."

"I'm glad. How's everything, Dan?"

"I haven't seen the patients, but my chief of staff was up waiting for me, and reports everything jake."

"That's all I wanted to know. Thanks, Dan. Oh, by the way, Flynn and Angelloti called on me again tonight."

"What's that!" The chief's voice was not unreminiscent of a St. Bernard dog's roar as he dashes out of his kennel at an unsuspecting tramp. "What are those two eggs up to? I told them to lay off you."

"They're doing that, Dan. They just called to apologize for disturbing me last night. They're delightful. They spent the evening with me. They only left a moment ago."

"The liquor must have run out."

"Oh, Dan!"

"I know those two. It would never occur to them to apologize to anybody if they didn't have a reason. It's just as I suspected, Lanny. They're going to hang on to this case on the quiet and trail you around."

An anguished thought popped into Lanny's agile brain. "Oh, Dan, suppose they took a notion to trail Stevie!"

"Hush! You don't have to paint me any picture, Lanny. When did these two busybodies call at your house?"

"At nine-fifteen."

"Wait a minute." Lanny waited a minute, and then McNamara said: "Stephen left here just about that time, so I guess we're safe tonight. And tomorrow I'll cover that loophole. I'm an ass not to have thought of it before. Good night."

He let himself into the house next night, with his latch-key, turned on the hall light and whistled. "Hello, everybody," he shouted. Nobody answered, so he hurried down to Nance's room. The door was open. He switched on the light and found a disordered bed with nobody in it. He searched the house thoroughly, only to discover he was alone in it; finally, on the living-room table he found a note:

Dear Chief: We think you mean well and we thank you for what you have done, but the dicks are watching this house. They trailed the doctor last night, but a friend of ours trailed them. Forgive us if we just can't trust any cop. Anyhow, it would be embarrassing for you if your men found us here. Good-by and good luck.

McNamara sat down. He was suddenly weak. So he hadn't fooled Flynn and Angelloti after all. The smart devils! Well, they might suspect all they pleased, but unless they had seen his guests and recognized Nance they could never prove anything. He wondered if Nance and her loyal friends had made a clean getaway.

The front door-bell rang and he went to answer it. A thin, bent man stood in the entrance, and even in the dim light from the hall McNamara knew him for an ex-convict in his prison suit of civilian clothes.

"Chief McNamara?" he queried huskily.

"Yes. I'm the chief."

"I got out of San Quentin this morning. I had a message for you, but I didn't want to come to headquarters to deliver it. Benny the Beetle told me to tell you to rest easy."

"Thanks, friend. Come in and rest easy yourself. Let's get acquainted," McNamara invited hospitably. In the clearer light of the living-room he saw that his visitor was far from being a well man. "What is it, kid?" he demanded with gruff kindness. "Hop— or T. B.?"

"The old coughin' sickness, chief. The prison directors shortened my term to let me out for treatment. As if I can get treatment anywhere," he added bitterly.

"Oh, yes, you can. I'm living alone here for the next thirty days, so I'll get a nurse in to take care of you, and you stay here."

The man looked at him suspiciously. "You mean it, chief?"

"What did Benny tell you about me?" he asked.

"He told me to trust you. He said you was one human being, even if you was a chief of police."

Dan changed the linen on Nance's bed, put the room in order, laid out a suit of pajamas and ordered his guest to bed.

"And now, me bold buckos," he reflected, "keep on trailing Dr. Burt to my house, if you feel like it."

He waited up until Stephen Burt arrived, and explained the situation to him. Stephen considered it a tremendous joke but commended his line of attack on Flynn and Angelloti.

"The man does need treatment very badly," he told the chief. "I'll send around a practical nurse early tomorrow morning to look after him, and I'll continue to call upon the poor devil nightly until further orders. We're both involved in a tricky game now and must play the hand through."

He was suddenly serious. "I do hope we haven't lost Nance, Dan. She's the most interesting psychological case I've ever seen."

"She ain't lost, but I'll bet a cookie she's well hid. But I'll locate her within twelve hours," he added, thinking of Ella Cates.

"I've run Nance's early history down since I saw you last, doc," he announced suddenly. "I got busy the other day and luck was with me. She's an heiress and her name is Penelope Gatlin. She got it in the nose by a baseball—a long fly into the bleachers. But I also discovered something else. It's a question whether she ain't just a natural nut. Her mother is. A religious fanatic—the sort that thinks it can cure a busted nose by faith. She led Gatlin a hell of a life."

"Did you meet her mother?"

"No, but I'm going to. I'll run her down easy enough."

Stephen sighed. "Oh, poor Nance! I'm afraid she's beyond my skill after all. A bad family history, Mac—very bad. There's a structural weakness in some families that never gets bred out, and I suspect poor Nance has an inheritance of mental instability from her mother."

"Well, with that busted nose, her inheritance and her hell-cat mother, she certainly had a fine start on the road to the foolish farm, didn't she, doc? Excuse me, there's the telephone."

Lanny was calling. "Dan," she quavered, "my house has been burglarized. They jimmied the back door, and for all I know the burglars are upstairs still. I'm watching the staircase—got my pistol covering it. Come over quick, Dan—please."

"Coming right away, Lanny." He hung up and faced Stephen. "Lanny has burglars. Into your car, boy, and we'll beat it over."

Lanny, very white and shaken, was in her living-room, pistol in hand, watching the stairs, when Mc-Namara and Stephen came noiselessly in the back door. The chief whipped out his pistol and went unhesitatingly up the stairs. Presently he called to them to come up.

They found him standing in the doorway leading into Lanny's guest-chamber. "Take a look at that," he ordered.

They looked. Lying in the bed, sound asleep, was Nance Belden!

McNamara switched off the light and softly closed the door. With his great head clasped in both huge hands, he went down the stairs to the living-room. "Doc," he pleaded, "who's loony now? I think I am because I'm seeing things that ain't in the book. Ochone, ochone, and wirra, wirra, the fairies have me in tow!" Lanny and Stephen laughed.

"Got to get her out of here," Dan McNamara decided. "Flynn and Angelloti finally got on her trail, no doubt about that—and it's a mighty cold trail those two dicks can't follow. I suspected this, and the note she left at my house confirms it. It's just the mercy of God that Flynn and Angelloti didn't happen to slip into my domicile and find the note. If they had I'd be sunk. They can suspect all they want to, but hanging it on to me is another pair of boots, as the French say."

"Why, they wouldn't dare invade their own chief's house," Lanny protested.

"They wouldn't? You don't know those two bozos like I do. They'd dare anything if they figured they could get away with it."

"Can't you give the miserable snoopers an office job?" Lanny demanded. She was faintly provoked at Daniel for his lack of initiative.

"Would you herd cows with a couple of horses that had won the Derby?"

"Oh!"

"Wake that psychopathic nuisance up, Lanny, and get her down here. I've got to find out things or go crazy. Besides, she hasn't had any dinner.

"Let the poor lamb sleep, Dan," pleaded Lanny.

"I need a lot of sleep myself and I can't get it until I know how, when, and where Nance and her gang made the getaway. Suppose Flynn and Angelloti let them make the getaway; suppose Flynn followed the men and Angelloti followed Nance? They'd do that; they wouldn't risk getting in Dutch with me by making the pinch as the gang came out of my house. They have some loyalty and a lot of common sense, and they know which side their bread is buttered on. When they take the girl they'll not turn her in to me. They'll waltz her straight back to San Quentin to the warden and let his men get the credit for recapturing her. All they want is the reward. Suppose they know she's here now and suppose they've seen me come here? Ouch! Murderation!"

"Have her down, Lanny," Stephen commanded in

his operating-room voice, and Lanny had no alternative save to obey. So presently Nance came down the
stairs with her. The girl was arrayed in an old wadded
dressing-gown of Lanny's, her hair was tousled, and
she yawned sleepily.

"Hello, Stevie, old darling; hello, Dan, you great
big beautiful thing. Here I am."

"Sit down," McNamara invited in honeyed accents.

So Nance sat down promptly—on his tremendous
knees—put her arm around his burly neck and kissed
him. "Now, don't get excited," she cooed. "I know
exactly what's burning you up, but you needn't worry.
One of the boys recognized Flynn and Angelloti. We
watched them through a hole in the curtain. They kept
circling the block in their car all the afternoon, and
when it was almost dark, we saw Flynn go into an
alley alongside a vacant house across the street. We
decided Angelloti had gone home for dinner. So we
telephoned Angelloti's house, and his wife said that
he was eating his dinner, and unless it was important
to call up in fifteen minutes. So we said it wasn't important, hung up and held a conference.

"We decided the back of the house wasn't guarded,
so we telephoned the boy friend that met us at the
yacht harbor that night, and he came and parked in the
next street. We went out your back door, leaving the
light in the front room burning, and shinnied over the
back fence. Some job for two members of the party,
I'll say. Once over the fence we had to prowl through

the back yard of the house that abuts against the rear
of your house—and a dog bit me, but not very hard.
We got in front and into the next street before anybody could come out and see what luck the dog had
had; our car was there and we beat it. We're pretty
sure nobody followed us, but we drove out to the park
first with our lights doused, and when we were sure
nobody was trailing us, the boys brought me here. We
jimmied your back door, Lanny dear; then the boys
said good-by to me for keeps. It seems you don't want
me associating with them any more, and they think
you're right about that, Dan."

"Did your men scout the street in front of this
house before pulling up in front of it?" asked Mc-
Namara sharply.

"Certainly. We circled the block twice."

"Feed our Nance, Lanny," McNamara urged happily. "She's a smart girl. How's the shoulder, dearie?"

"Fine. It'll be O.K. in another week."

"So am I." Mr. McNamara grinned horribly.
"Flynn's home eating his dinner now, and Angelloti
must be on guard in that alley. I'm going to mistake
Angelloti for a suspicious character, lurking there in
the dark—and put a mark on him so I can recognize
him later. He just can't stand to mix it with me, and
get recognized, of course, so when he runs I'll fire in
the air. He'll know who I am, but he'll never suspect
I know who he is.

He bade them good night and hurried away in a taxi.
A block from his home he alighted and came on foot

down the side of the street opposite his own house. He was whistling softly as he came abreast Angelloti's hiding-place, where he turned at right angles, apparently with the intention of crossing in the middle of the street to his own house. A step from the curb he halted, turned, bent his head in a listening attitude, then stepped resolutely into the alley.

"Who's there?" he demanded. Receiving no answer, he got out a small flash-light; he seemed to have some difficulty flashing it on, for he cursed softly, and suddenly a beam from the flash-light illumined his own face for an instant, but long enough, he decided, to permit the watchful Angelloti to recognize him. The alley was empty, but in a little garden strip about two feet wide a large syringa bush grew, and instinct warned the chief that his prey was crouched behind it. So he walked past it, and, as he had anticipated, a hand reached out and snatched the flash-light from him. As he turned, one of his stout legs was jerked from under him by a man crouching low; so, before permitting himself to topple backward, McNamara dropped his good right arm to the level of his knee and swung a short, stabbing punch. He felt a cheek-bone and the side of a nose; so he punched again, a little higher up, and then fell over backward. Instantly his assailant rose and fled like a roe.

"Halt! I'm an officer," McNamara shouted, and fired into the air. But the running man did not even hesitate.

In the morning the chief sent for Angelloti for a report on a certain case, and was charmed to note a faintly lemonish spot on the Italian's left cheek and a very noticeable iridescence under the left eye. The chief grinned. "What does the other fellow look like, Angie?" he queried innocently. "He couldn't have been more'n a fly-weight or he'd have done more damage! How come you let some runt one-two you like that?"

"It was a dame I picked up for solicitin'," Angelloti lied with the glibness of long practice.

Following some discussion of the report McNamara dismissed him, and sat down to decide what to do with Nance Belden. That Flynn and Angelloti were keeping his house under surveillance he knew now; undoubtedly they would enter his house at the earliest favorable opportunity.

The chief wondered what he would do if he stood in the shoes of his two detectives. "I'd wait for a night when I wouldn't be disturbed for a couple of hours," he decided. "What night would that be? Why, Thursday night, when the board of police commissioners meet and I am in attendance there. Stephen will make his usual early evening call—and as soon as he leaves the house those two cuties will slip into it. The cellar door, of course. I'll make it easy for them. I'll leave the door unlocked."

He concluded that until then Nance would be safe at Lanny's house. In the meantime, however, he must arrange to get her out of the city at an early date. The detectives were both absolutely satisfied Lanny had once given Nance sanctuary for a brief period; trust them, therefore, to keep an eye on Lanny's house.

He had in his office a telephone line that did not connect with the private exchange system in the Central Station, so he called Lanny on this phone at Dr. Burt's office now.

"Dan speaking, Lanny. Tomorrow morning you had better buy our pet nuisance a lot of clothes, so she'll be all ready to get out of town when I send for her. I think I'll have to fly her out and down to Tia Juana."

"What will she do there?"

"I don't know. We'll think about that when she gets there. At least my two dicks won't be there, and Tia Juana is one place where that saddle nose of hers won't surprise anybody. And when she acts rough and tough in Tia Juana nobody will pay any attention to her. They have experts down there in that line."

"I'll think that Tia Juana stunt over," Lanny decided. "It has possibilities. Is there a good hospital there?"

"I don't think so. Why?"

"You numskull, Dan McNamara! We have to find a quiet hospital where we can have her poor nose operated on."

"Well, if we can get her beezer restored and change that black bob of hers to a movie-tone gold, she could take Flynn and Angelloti out to dinner, and they'd never suspect her."

"Stevie says her nose must be operated on first. Her

present state of dissociated personality probably
started in an inferiority complex, and the inferiority
complex probably arose out of the knowledge that her
nose made her unlovely. When it's safe to bring her
back to this city, Stevie will take her soul out and look
at it, dust it off, put it back and do a Little Jack
Horner."

"Can he do that?" McNamara's heavy voice was
freighted with awe.

"He can, provided he can find a starting point for
his investigations into her past life. There is always
a reason for a dissociated personality. The ground for
the mental shock that causes it is usually prepared
long before the psychosis occurs. Rebellious thoughts,
unhappiness, brooding—all these eventually have a
serious effect upon sensitive and highly intelligent people and particularly women of the hysterical type."

"All women are hysterical," McNamara said with
conviction.

"You're a dear booby, Dan. Eight women out of
ten can throw a fit of hysterics as easily as you'd break
an egg, particularly if there is a man to be impressed.
They never simulate hysterics to impress a woman,
however, because they know better. However, there
are women who have hysterics that are real, but it has
been the experience of this office that most of these
are just a trifle balmy—neurotics."

"Well, you get our girl a trousseau and warn her
to keep away from the window and not to answer the

door-bell, or do any telephoning, or leave the house until she has my permission. I don't expect she'll obey, so tonight when you go home have some hysterics to impress her."

"Dan, dear, I couldn't. I'm hard as a picnic egg. Did you stage your little comedy after leaving us last night?"

"I did—and it worked out exactly."

"Good gracious. Well, I'm busy. Good-by."

CHAPTER NINE

NANCE BELDEN'S personalities were a source of keen professional interest to Lanny, who regretted that for the present Dr. Burt was unable to share her observations with her. She as yet had had no opportunity for ascertaining anything regarding the girl's past history, but she had a suspicion that Nance had had advantages superior to most girls. Her hands were the first thing (with the exception of her wrecked nose) that Lanny had noticed. They were soft, shapely, small, and well kept, decidedly not the hands of a factory girl. While her vocabulary was a trifle "salty," running at times to the idiom of the ill-bred and ignorant, her voice was soft, with well-bred intonations. Her clothing, on the occasion of her visit to Stephen Burt's office, had been, in Lanny's judgment, in splendid taste; rich, but not flashy, up to the mode but not beyond it. Then, too, Nance had a slow, leisurely walk; she knew how to enter a room, she was sure of herself at all times without display assurance. To Lanny the girl, in her abandoned moments, appeared to be amateurish, a bit of a show-off, unreal.

Thus far she had observed the girl only in this phase of her personality. She was amazed, therefore, on coming home from the office after her conversation with McNamara, to find her a complete changeling. As she entered the house she caught the odor of cooking, and going into the kitchen she discovered Nance, in one of Lanny's kitchen aprons, preparing dinner.

"Good evening, Lanny dear," she saluted her hostess. "It occurred to me it must be a very great trial to you, coming home night after night from the office tired, and having to prepare dinner for yourself. I'm sure you're too tired most of the time to prepare more than a very sketchy meal, and that isn't good for you." She smiled. "So I thought I'd have a nice dinner for you."

"Now, I call that real sweet, Nance."

"My name isn't Nance, Lanny. It's Penelope."

"Penelope what?"

"Penelope Gatlin. Silly old Lanny, how could you forget?"

"You've placed your finger on my dread secret, Penelope. When I'm tired my memory fails me."

Lanny knew that during the day a psychological door had opened and Nance Belden, otherwise personality B, the abnormal, had walked through it and emerged Penelope Gatlin, or personality A, the normal. Also, she knew now that Penelope Gatlin probably had more or less amnesia for her former personality as Nance Belden. Lanny had heard Dr. Burt discuss such rare cases, and she glowed with pride in the knowledge that at last he had secured a perfect specimen.

"I decided we wouldn't have broiled lamb chops, Lanny," the girl went on brightly, "so I've made a ragout."

"You mean, in good old Americanese, you've concocted an Irish stew."

"You're so amusing, Lanny. A stew, of course. The difference between a stew and a ragout is entirely geographic. A ragout in France, an Irish stew in the United States."

"Have you lived in France?"

"Eight years, Lanny. Went to school in Switzerland and learned French there."

"Are your people French?"

"I think I was there alone." The girl appeared puzzled. "I don't remember my mother, but I had a father. He was such a dear, but he's dead."

"Were you happy there?"

"No, I was perfectly miserable."

"Why?"

"Because my father wasn't with me. We'd been such pals."

"But you must have lived with somebody."

"There was Laurette, the cook, and Babette, the maid."

"Did you graduate?"

"No, I left school when father died. He was killed in a motor accident en route to Europe. I've always had a feeling he was coming over to see his Penelope. He loved me very much, Lanny. He was adorable. He

used to tell me that I was all that made his life bear-
able. Somebody—I forget who—told me he wasn't
my real father, that I was a foundling he adopted. I
wouldn't believe that at first, but when I read his will
I knew it was so."

"What sort of woman was his wife—or did he have
one?"

"I haven't the slightest idea, but I remember the
will stated very positively that he had settled with
her, that she had accepted the settlement in full satisfaction of her dower rights, and he made my income
from the trust just sufficient to support me decently
until I should come of age. He said in his will that
he did this not because of any lack of affection for
me, but because if he made me an excessive allowance,
his divorced wife would have control of it during my
minority. He must have despised her."

"Well, if she could have control of your income
during your minority, she must have been your
adopted mother," the practical Lanny reasoned. "And
you must have lived with her following the divorce.
That's why you didn't see your father in Europe. You
must have been there with your foster mother. Laurette, the cook, and Babette, the maid, argue an establishment. Do you remember everything that has happened to you since that day Dan McNamara brought
you to Dr. Burt's office?"

"Vaguely."

"Ever have funny thoughts about it?"

The girl stared at her shrewdly. "How strange that you should ask that question, Lanny. I do have funny thoughts. Sometimes I'm horrified at the memory and could die of shame; at other times it seems perfectly all right, but those are the times when I've been nervous and sleepless; sometimes I think there's something wrong with me, because people often refer to me as Nance Belden and to things I've done and which I know very well I haven't done. And yet it seems to me sometimes as if I had—just a wraith of memory, like an old dream. But still I'm strong and healthy."

"But a little given to spells of nervousness?"

"I'm moody." The girl seemed interested in herself to an unusual degree. "Some days I like to do things that are perfectly intolerable to me on other days. Some days I'm so democratic I could go out to dinner with a garbage man—other times I can't bear to be with anybody but nice people." She sighed and turned to inspect her savory ragout. "I wish I knew what I wanted in life and I wish I knew somebody that wanted me. Of course I can pay my way through life, but it's terrible to be lonely, Lanny."

She faced Lanny again. "Now, when I decided to cast myself on your hospitality, Lanny, it seemed to me the most natural thing in the world to do. But today I'm covered with confusion. I've deliberately imposed myself upon your peace and privacy."

"Listen here, Penny, my dear. You aren't the only lonely woman in this world. Believe it or not, the first spring buttercup isn't a bit more welcome in old lady Lanning's house than you are."

The lost one beamed upon her. "I believe that, Lanny. Oh, Lanny, when I'm happy I'm so happy, and when I'm wretched I'm so wretched."

"You think too much about that nose of yours."

The girl's hand flew to that organ (automatically, Lanny thought) as if she would hide it. "Isn't it *terrible?*" she quavered. "I'm so ugly nobody can ever love me."

"Quit that," Lanny commanded in her most ferocious manner. "If I hadn't found you lovable I wouldn't have you in my house this minute. I'd turn you over to Flynn and Angelloti. By the way," she continued, "how did you get that sock on the beezer?"

"Father took me to a baseball game and a long drive flew into the bleachers and struck me on the nose. Lanny, you mustn't use slang. It isn't polite."

"I wrap myself around a highball when I'm tired or want to be sociable, and I smoke cigarettes," Lanny protested. "I suppose a perfect lady wouldn't do those things, either?"

"A perfect lady may without marring her perfection, old fuss-budget. That's a matter of personal liberty, and only becomes distressing when carried to excess. But there's no excuse for a highly intelligent and cultured woman to employ the language of the street."

"I have my human moments," Lanny excused herself meekly.

"I'll set the table in the dining-room. Won't you order some flowers? And Lanny—I'll do something for you some day."

"For instance."

"Well, have you ever been to Europe?"

"Certainly not."

"Then I'll take you."

"I accept the nomination. In return I'll do something else for you. I'll have that nose of yours split open, the shattered bone of the bridge scraped out and a cute little piece of pliable cartilage whittled off one of your spare ribs, and grafted into your funny nose to form a new bridge. Then the doctor will sew your nose together again over it—"

"What's the difference between having a nose like a Pekingese and a makeshift with a big scar on it, I'd like to know?"

"Oh, there won't be any scar, dearie. The surgeon will cut a strip of epidermis off your forehead, and, without detaching it from your forehead, bring the flap down, drape it over your new scarred nose and graft it there. It will grow and cover the scar, and when everything's lovely, that skin connection with your forehead will be severed and the ragged edges trimmed and presently nature will do the rest. Six months after the operation I'll defy anybody but an expert to discover you've got a custom-made nose."

The girl's eyes shone. "Is it true, Lanny, is it true? It's so hard to believe in miracles."

"Science pulls 'em off daily, my dear."

Nance changed the subject. "Here, here, we're gabbling like a pair of geese. The linen, woman, where's the linen? Off with your hat and coat. While you're getting it I'll run upstairs and get your mules."

"After dinner I must do some more pumping," thought Lanny. "The information will be invaluable to Stephen. Strange case! Total amnesia sometimes, only partial amnesia at others. Dreadful mixture."

CHAPTER TEN

WHEN Dan McNamara came home about midnight from the regular weekly meeting of the police commission, he found his ex-convict guest up and waiting for him. "I had two burglars here tonight, about ten o'clock, chief," he announced.

The chief sat down and loaded his pipe. "I was expecting them, my boy. Did they ask you any questions?"

"No. They just searched the house. I don't think they touched anything except the lip-stick on the bureau over there," he said.

"Did they take the lip-stick?" Dan asked.

"They didn't take it, they looked at it."

McNamara sighed. The case was getting a little thick for him when it became complicated with lip-sticks. He went to the telephone and got Stephen Burt out of bed.

"Did a certain party, while a guest at my house, ask you to bring out a lip-stick when you called in the course of your professional duties, doctor?"

"Oh, yes."

"Thanks. Good night." McNamara hung up and went to the room lately occupied by Nance Belden

On the bureau he found a lip-stick. "Vanity is always the undoing of a crook," he sighed, and went to bed, greatly troubled in his mind at what was, to him, indubitable knowledge that Flynn and Angelloti, even though they had failed to find their quarry, must be convinced, beyond the shadow of a doubt, that he had harbored an escaped convict in his home.

He passed a sleepless night, but he did some solid thinking, so there was no lost time. He had hoped, by providing this sick convict as an excuse for Dr. Burt's nightly visits, to throw Flynn and Angelloti off the scent—and now the scent was hotter than ever.

"Now, what will they do? They're morally certain she went to Lanny's house the night she escaped and that Lanny got her out of there in the nick of time and took her here. Now that she's escaped them here they may suspect she'd doubled back to Lanny's house. Murderation! However, those two dicks will never bother her without fortifying themselves with a search-warrant. They'd be too afraid of me. But with a search-warrant and the girl to show for their pains they'll have me foul. I couldn't open my mouth—if they bring the girl into headquarters I'll have to give them a cheer and congratulate them."

He decided Flynn and Angelloti would sleep on their evidence and the suspicions it had roused, compare notes in the morning, and decide upon a course of action. They would have to adduce some nominal evidence to support their suspicion before the district attorney would consent to issue the search-warrant, for a search-warrant is not issued lightly. In the morning they would induce some stool-pigeon to tell the district attorney that he had seen Nance Belden's face at the window of Lanny's home. Possibly they might induce the patrolman on that beat to stretch the truth a little.

"I can't get Nance out of Lanny's house tonight, and I can't get her out in daylight tomorrow, but I *must* get her out tomorrow night," he decided. "But how?"

He was at his office at eight next morning. At eight-thirty he looked into the detectives' room and saw Flynn and Angelloti in profound conference. Half an hour later he stepped out of a taxi two blocks from Lanny's house, and when the cab had disappeared, he made his way to the house and was admitted by Lanny.

"Nance has got to make a clean getaway," he assured her earnestly, "because tonight Flynn and his pal may come with a search-warrant. The district attorney will probably call me up before he issues it, and I'll have to tell him to go ahead and issue it, in order to allay suspicion. Now, here are a half a dozen harmless hand-grenades that burst on impact. Three of them are tear bombs and three are stink bombs.

"Now, I'll tell you exactly how they'll make the pinch. They'll not come during the day, because they'll know you aren't at home and that Nance wouldn't answer the bell anyhow. But tonight, one of them will ring the front door-bell and shove the search-warrant under your nose and step inside. The other will, in the meantime, have gone around to your back door to prevent the girl's escape in that direction. There's a cement floor around your kitchen door, is there not?"

"Yes? Well, when the door-bell rings, you answer it. That will be Nance's tip to peek out the second-story window and lob three bombs down on the cement beside whoever she sees standing there. They explode with a sound like a gunshot and diffuse their gas almost instantly over a considerable area. Now, whichever one goes to the back door will never be expecting a citizen to shower this sort of bombs down on him, because they are not accessible to citizens; so he will think they're electric-light bulbs tossed down to scare him away. By the way, have Nance toss one electric-light bulb down first, and then follow with two tear bombs —here, I'll make a mark with my pencil on the tear bombs. Before he realizes what has happened he'll be weeping like Niobe and unable to see anything in the darkness.

"But bear this in mind, Lanny. He'll not desert his post. He'll think he's been blinded so Nance can slip past him and go over the back fence, so he'll hug the back door and be ready to grab her when she comes. He'll stick it out. That's the time Nance must drop a stink bomb beside him.

"Meanwhile, the man in front will hear the explosions. If the one in back cries out, the one in front will figure he has been shot and will run through your house to help him. As he opens the back door his pal will grab him. You must follow at his heels and shut and bolt the door instantly, or you'll get yours, too. There will be a momentary struggle between Flynn and Angelloti in the dark, because the front-door man will think he has the scoundrel that hurled the bombs; and by the time they discover each other's identity, the front-door man will be as sightless and ill as the back-door man.

"Nance, a word to you now."

"My name is Penelope Gatlin, Dan."

"My error. Penelope, the instant you drop those first two bombs, shut down the window. And, remember, all the lights in the rear of the house and particularly in the kitchen must be turned off. When the front-door man is struggling with his pal and Lanny has closed the door, her scream will be your cue to open the window again, just long enough to lay the rest of your eggs on the scrimmage. You must be dressed for the street and have some money in your pocket. . . . Got any?"

"No."

"Here's two hundred."

"I'll send you my check. Thanks." And she took the money. Her manner had undergone a subtle change.

"Immediately after tossing the last of the bombs, close the window and beat it downstairs and out the front door. I'll leave a closed coupé, with the motor running, parked at the curb across the street. Can you drive?"

"I can drive, Dan."

"Very well, then. Climb into the car and beat it."

"Beat it where?"

"Los Angeles, San Diego, anywhere. Keep on going, and when you get there send me a wire to the Central Station merely giving your address. Then lay low until somebody comes after you. Keep off the street. Lanny, you must disguise her nose. Clamp a wadding of cotton and a neat dressing over it to hide the dish in it. Any lady is liable to have an injury to her nose and wear a dressing on it. Now, is everything understood?"

Nance nodded and Lanny's silence gave consent. "You'll probably get a whiff of what's good for Flynn and Angelloti," McNamara advised Lanny, "but you'll get over it. When you lob over the last of your rotten eggs, Penelope, do not breathe, and close your eyes tightly until you have closed the window again. Then —out of the house like a shot. This plan of mine is fool-proof if followed absolutely, but it's you for San Quentin again if it isn't, my brave lassie, and all the chiefs of police in town cannot help you then."

"Thank you, sir," said Nance politely and with quiet dignity. "You are most kind to take this trouble for a stranger, and I shall never forget it." And she held out her hand.

McNamara looked in puzzlement at Lanny. "What's happened to her?" he demanded.

"I'll explain to you sometime. You're a brilliant chief of police and you've figured everything out to a gnat's eyelash for Penelope, but what's going to happen to me?"

"The concoction of the plan I've just outlined has given me brain fag, Lanny. It's cost me a night's sleep. I don't know what's going to happen to you and I don't much care. You're a smart woman, and you can figure a way out of your end of the mess."

"I wish I could relish that compliment," Lanny retorted dryly. "However, if you think I'm not going to laugh myself sick over this you're a poor judge of women. Good-by, you old crook, and God bless you. Kiss him, Penelope."

A becoming modesty caused the girl to hesitate just a little, then she came to the chief and implanted a most ladylike kiss on his blue jowl. "You're very kind, Mr. McNamara," she assured him again.

"Cripes," he muttered and went off.

Dan McNamara's estimate of the ability of Detective-Sergeants Flynn and Angelloti did them no injustice; indeed, they proved even smarter than their chief credited them with being. Angelloti's adventure with Dan McNamara they passed over as an unavoidable accident; Angelloti was certain McNamara had not recognized him. He felt certain McNamara had no suspicion that his house was under surveillance, although Flynn had mental reservations on that point, for the Irish are a psychic race.

After watching Dr. Burt enter and leave the chief's house on Thursday night, when they knew the chief would not be home until midnight, they decided to investigate. The unlocked cellar door gave them pause; Flynn whispered that he was always suspicious of things that came too easy. They crept upstairs and found Dan McNamara's ex-convict guest reading in bed. Both detectives recognized him, so while Angelloti guarded him Flynn made a hurried but thorough search of the premises. They were not in the house more than five minutes.

"We've been like two pups, chasing our tails," Angelloti complained when they met at their car. "The chief's up to his old tricks, babying a convict with the con, and that's the bird Dr. Burt is calling to treat."

"The girl's been there, just the same, Amadeo, my boy. There was a lip-stick on the bureau, and that's something old lady McNamara don't use. And I found a roll of adhesive, the heel of a roll of bandage and a soiled sheet with some bloodstains on it in the dirty clothes basket in the bathroom."

Angelloti was convinced. "Where did she go?"

"She might have doubled back to that old nurse's house again, but I doubt that because she knows that's risky."

"Well, let's give Miss Lanning's house a prowl, anyhow."

Flynn was one of those hearty fellows who will try

anything twice, so they went immediately to Lanny's house. The lights in front were out when they arrived, so Flynn pussyfooted around to the rear of the cottage to see if any lights were lighted there. Finding none, he listened for possible voices. Hearing none, he cautiously lifted the lid off Lanny's garbage can and bent his flash-light on it. He was rewarded for his courage by finding a stained bandage with clipped adhesive tape clinging to it. This telltale evidence he carried around to Angelloti; they entered their car, drove a block and inspected the clue in the light of the dash lamp. Then they silently shook hands.

"Nothing is ever lost if you know where it is," Flynn rejoiced. "I'm going to get my missus a winter coat with my half of the reward. We'll bone the district attorney for a search-warrant tomorrow, and tomorrow night when the old lady get's home, we'll make the pinch."

"Shall we pinch her as an accessory?"

"Amadeo, my boy, unless you're looking hard for something, it's a mistake to see too much or know too much. This Lanning woman is a friend of the chief's. As far as the public ever need know we picked the girl up on the street."

Angelloti nodded his acquiescence; they got the search-warrant on the strength of that soiled bandage, and at nine o'clock that night arrived in their car. Flynn went to the back door and posted himself there; and Angelloti rang the front door-bell. A light was switched on in the hall presently, and Lanny, dressed for the street, opened the door six inches. Angelloti had his foot in it in a flash.

"Detective-Sergeant Angelloti of the Central Station, Miss Lanning. I have here a search-warrant, giving me legal right to search your house and secure the person of Nance Belden, an escaped convict from San Quentin penitentiary. Read it an' weep!"

"You take your big flat foot out of my door and stay outside until I've read this purported search-warrant or I'll shoot your foot off," Lanny informed him coldly. Angelloti withdrew his foot promptly, Lanny closed the door, and he could see her faintly through the curtained glass, reading.

"Come in," she invited—and at that moment the electric-light bulb tossed out the upper window by Nance exploded with a loud report. "What's that?" Angelloti cried, instantly alert. A still louder explosion reverberated in the back yard; then the voice of Flynn crying: "Hey, stop or I'll shoot."

"Tried slippin' her out the back door, eh?" Angelloti exulted, and dashed through the house, with Lanny at his heels. As he went out the kitchen door, Lanny slammed and bolted it behind him, and then, even as Dan McNamara had predicted, Nature took her course. Nance dropped the remainder of the bombs and came dashing down the stairs. "Good-by, Lanny, darling," she cried happily. "We'll meet again." Lanny switched off the hall light, and Nance was through the front door and gone. Across the street two coupés stood at the curb, the motors of both turning over slowly.

Alternately the girl's finger was pointed at each car. "My—mother—told—me—to—take—this—one," she murmured, and when through the aid of this childhood formula, she had made her decision, she leaped into the coupé of Messrs. Flynn and Angelloti and went rapidly away. Lanny, watching her from the darkened doorway, saw that she had taken the wrong car, but was afraid to cry out and warn her. So she did the next best thing. She locked her front door behind her, climbed into the other car and drove downtown to a late motion-picture show. She carried the search-warrant with her and while enjoying the show tore it into little bits.

Of the weeping, the groaning, the burning sensations in the eyelids, the bewilderment, the groping, vomiting, cursing, and despair of Messrs. Flynn and Angelloti, nothing need be said. Suffice that Angelloti felt his way out of the gassed area and about two minutes after Lanny's departure, stationed himself on her front steps, while the valiant Flynn, dying a thousand deaths, stuck manfully at his post, leaning up against the kitchen door, enduring for duty's sake. Convinced they had Nance Belden cornered, they waited for the night wind to dissipate the gas. Angelloti ceased to weep about half an hour after escaping from the gassed area, but continued to gag for an hour. About ten-thirty he was able to see, so he rang Lanny's bell repeatedly, but received no answer. Then he noticed that their car was missing, so he summoned the martyred Flynn around front and told him the worst.

"Don't speak to me," Flynn commanded passionately. "I'm dead! Hunt up an all-night drug store an' phone for a taxi."

"This," Angelloti hissed, "is Dan McNamara's work. Where would they get the bombs if he didn't swipe 'em out of the police arsenal?"

Flynn commenced to sob as he considered the barren fruits of his enormous sacrifice.

"Amadeo, swear to me, by our common faith, that, come what will, blow high, blow low, come sickness or sorrow, happiness or health, you'll never lay off this job until we've landed that—that—that huzzy."

"Right! I swear." Angelloti's voice trembled with the sincerity of his purpose.

The respective wives of the worthy pair telephoned down to the chief of the detectives next morning and informed him that their husbands were confined to bed with influenza. It might not be amiss, also, to state that Lanny came home in a taxi about twelve-thirty, and finding the front door free of Angelloti and the neighborhood ozone quite restored to normalcy, retired to her bed and passed almost at once into dreamless and untroubled sleep.

It was not a police car in which Nance had escaped, but the private vehicle of Detective-Sergeant Flynn, and its loss troubled him until the car was found, abandoned, out in the Mission, about twenty-four hours later. A glance at the speedometer comforted Flynn. The car had been driven six miles. In company with Angelloti (both now happily recovered from their terrible experience) he drove in the same car from Lanny's house, via the most direct route, to the point where a patrolman had picked up the car; thence via the route followed by the patrolman when he came off duty and drove the car to the Central Station garage and reported it. The mileage was six and two-tenth miles!

"She's holed up within a block or two of where she left the car," Flynn decided.

"Not such a cold trail, after all," Angelloti exulted. "We'll just have to patrol the neighborhood in our off moments. I'm sure the girl doesn't know she swiped your car, and that she gave us a clue to follow her."

"If crooks didn't make mistakes and give us the breaks, my boy, you and I wouldn't be where we are," Flynn reminded him. "I think it might be a good idea to interview the druggist in the neighborhood and see if she's been in to buy a new lip-stick."

A round of the neighboring drug stores, however, proved barren of a new lead, and as they had other matters claiming their attention, they were forced to abandon the search for that day.

Dan McNamara was much too intelligent to make inquiries of the assistant district attorney who had issued the search-warrant, but when informed that Flynn and Angelloti were down with flu he called up Lanny at Stephen's office, and received a meticulous report. "You say the girl fled in the car my dicks arrived in?" he queried. "That's terrible. A description of the car must have been broadcast to all outlying police and the surrounding country stations immediately by Flynn and Angelloti, and Nance will be picked up somewhere down state."

"We've done our damnedest," Lanny replied cheerfully. "Angels can do no more. I borrowed the car you left out front. It's in a garage. I'll send you the claim check."

For a week, the chief waited for news of Nance Belden, but no news came through beyond some gossip around the Central Station that the car had been driven but three miles and then abandoned—for which evidence that the Almighty was still on his side the worthy fellow was grateful.

So Nance was still in the city! McNamara's mind worked so automatically he did not even have to tell himself that, undoubtedly, she had taken sanctuary within a short distance of the spot where she had abandoned Flynn's car, nor did he have to remind himself that Flynn and Angelloti would come to the same conclusion. He had no difficulty in ascertaining the spot where the car had been recovered.

"Folsom Street and Sixteenth, eh?" he reflected. "Residential—flat buildings and cheap apartment-houses, cheap rooming-houses and working-men's hotels. No, she wouldn't go to one of those. Nut that she is, she has class—and she had two hundred dollars in her possession. She's holed up with a friend. What friend? Why, Ella Cates, of course."

He had already secured Ella Cates's address from the banker in San José. However, he realized it would not be wise to call upon her and run the risk of having Flynn or Angelloti run across him in the neighborhood or see him entering Ella Cates's house. The obvious thing, therefore, was to cast about for a job in another part of the city and see that both detectives were assigned to it. If he sent them out of the city for a day or two they might suspect his purpose and have some other dick friend of theirs shadow him during their absence.

While he was considering where he could dispose of them, the president of the Security Trust Company in San José rang up.

"Miss Penelope Gatlin has just been in the bank, chief," he told McNamara. "She has purchased a letter of credit for ten thousand dollars and has withdrawn in cash the remainder of the funds on deposit to the credit of her checking account, amounting to eleven hundred dollars."

"Is she in the bank now?"

'Yes."

"Have one of your clerks follow her. Give him some expense money—I'll be responsible for its repayment. And when you get his report please telephone me."

At three-thirty the banker telephoned again. "She purchased a ticket to San Francisco on one of the busses leaving here at three-fifteen. She spent two hours shopping."

The busses, McNamara knew, entered the city via

Mission Street; the bus depot was at Fifth and Mission streets. Ella Cates lived on Howard Street, between Fifteenth and Sixteenth. Howard Street runs between Mission and Folsom—and Flynn's car had been found abandoned at Sixteenth and Folsom. Nance was smart. She had left the car a block from Ella Cates's home and walked there. McNamara reasoned the incoming bus would drop the girl off at Sixteenth and Mission streets—a regular stop—and she would then make her way to the Cates woman's house.

He glanced at his watch. He had an hour and a half to intercept her; for that hour and a half he must have Flynn and Angelloti in another section of the city. To his annoyance, he discovered they were out on a detail, so he decided he would have to risk it, called a taxi and drove to Ella Cates's address. He discovered it to be a cheap wooden apartment-house, but the directory in the vestibule gave him no information as to which apartment Ella Cates lived in, so he rang the landlady's bell, and the door opened to admit him. To his inquiry regarding Mrs. Cates, he was informed that she had moved to parts unknown a week before, nor could she give him any clue to aid him in discovering her.

As he came out of the apartment house he glanced warily around and was amused to observe Detective Angelloti leaning against a cigar stand across the street. He was certain the detective had recognized him, for Angelloti immediately turned his back. The chief walked up to Mission Street, boarded a street-car and was at the bus terminus two minutes before the bus on which Nance had left San José rolled in. But Nance was not among the passengers that alighted.

McNamara chuckled. Flynn and Angelloti would waste a great deal of time watching that apartment house in vain. Nance, discovering Ella Cates had moved, had sought quarters elsewhere. What puzzled McNamara, however, was the girl's failure to communicate with him or Lanny; and he knew now that she did not intend to. The fact that she had purchased a letter of credit was proof that she intended leaving the country, and the more the excellent fellow contemplated this impending move the more inclined was he to regard it as a not unmixed blessing.

The more he thought the matter over, the more inclined did he become to take a practical and policeman-like view of the situation. While Nance remained in San Francisco she would be a constant menace to himself and Lanny; if captured she might, during one of her uncontrolled moments, consider it a great joke to tell the world how she had been enabled to escape capture so long.

"I can't baby the world," he decided. "I'll let her go. She'll probably live abroad, and when her letter of credit is gone she may remember who she is long enough to draw more checks. I can always get a line on her through the bank, and if Steve and Lanny still insist on salvaging this nut I'll tell them where to find her. Me, I'm through. If I keep this pace up I'll be as big a nut as she is."

CHAPTER ELEVEN

THERE is more than a modicum of truth in the ancient adage, "Out of sight, out of mind." Dan McNamara lived a very full life; and when Nance Belden had definitely passed beyond his ken and he knew himself safe at last from the prying of Messrs. Flynn and Angelloti into his private affairs, he forgot the girl, for pressing matters of great importance claimed his attention and he required more first-class assistance than he was receiving. He resolved, therefore, to give Flynn and Angelloti a week in which to make up their minds they had lost the trail; then to call them in.

On the sixth day, however, he received information that the doughty pair were still as busy as two pups with a feather duster. A beautiful lady called on him at his office and told him so.

"And who might you be?" he demanded.

"I'm Susan Engelbright."

"I am not aware that I have the pleasure of your acquaintance, Miss Engelbright."

"You haven't. I was sent up from Oakland."

"Oh! Alias Sapphire Susie; I've heard of you lately."

"Perhaps. I hocked three twelve-carat sapphire rings to raise money to beat the rap, and the papers called me Sapphire Susie after that."

"I see you got them out of hock again, Susie."

The girl nodded. "Nance Belden got them out for me."

"Part of the bargain for smuggling that letter out of San Quentin for her, I suppose."

"Never mind what it was for." Sapphire Susie smiled archly and unafraid. "I earned it and she kept her word."

"Check or cash?" McNamara was frightened. If Sapphire Susie had been given a check then she knew Nance Belden's real name and the name of her bank. And that would be fatal.

"I don't know. I gave her the pawn tickets and she brought back the rings."

"When?" He was relieved.

"A week ago tomorrow."

"And you say Detective-Sergeant Flynn has been giving you a bad half-hour?"

"Yes, he has."

"Well, that's his business. Nance Belden escaped from San Quentin, and naturally he's interested in apprehending her. You were recognized by the guard at the main gate two weeks before Nance escaped. Miss Lanning, a friend of the Belden girl, had visited the prisoner that day, and since Miss Lanning was the only visitor Nance Belden had in San Quentin, naturally she

was suspected of carrying a letter for delivery to the
men who helped Nance escape. You rode down to
Greenbrae with Miss Lanning, and she slipped the letter
to you, of course. Flynn knows that. But why do you
come to me with your tale of woe?"

"I've run straight since getting out of the pen. I
served my time and I want to be let alone—that's why!
Flynn told me that if I didn't come through and tell
him where he could find Nance Belden he'd see to it
that something nasty happened to me. I don't know
where Nance Belden is. And I want protection from
Flynn."

"You seem pretty sure of me, don't you?"

"Well, Nance told me that you were one human
being. And I called on Miss Lanning last night to
tell her to warn Nance that the dicks were after her,
and Miss Lanning told me to see you about it. She
said you'd see I got a square deal."

"She did so, now? How did Miss Lanning treat you
otherwise?"

"She kissed me and gave me a hundred dollars and
told me to be as good as I could. That old girl is sure a
darling."

"Did you ask her for the hundred?"

"Of course not."

The chief eyed her owlishly, for he distrusted Sapphire Susie and wondered if she might not be working
in the interests of Flynn and Angelloti.

"This is interesting," he admitted heavily. "Of

course I only keep in touch with the upper office through the captain of detectives. If he set Flynn on this job he should have interviewed you a couple of weeks ago. Seems to me he has overlooked a good bet. If he'd had you under surveillance a week ago he'd have picked up Nance Belden when she came to you to deliver the rings. Flynn's a crackerjack detective," he added sadly, "but this looks as if he's slipping."

"That bird don't slip very far, take it from me, chief. He met me on the street the day before yesterday and noticed I was wearing my big ring and my eardrops. 'Hello, kid,' he says, 'I see you got your sapphires on again.' I says to him, 'Fall dead, you bum,' and walked on. And the next night he came up to my room. 'Nance Belden got them sapphires out of hock for you, Susie, my dear,' he says kindly. 'I want that frail. Where is she?' "

"And you wouldn't tell him, even if you could?"

"That's a fact. I wouldn't snitch on the girl."

"You wouldn't expect me to interfere in the work of a detective-sergeant when he appears to be doing a good job, would you, Susie? But I give you my word, Susie, that if you run straight in this city I'll see to it that you're not harassed. Of course you helped Nance Belden to escape from San Quentin, and I know it, but I can't prove it; if I could I'd put you in the bird-cage this minute. And I'll not pull Flynn off the case, although if he gets too rough I'll stop him."

"He's got me scared to death," Sapphire Susie de-

clared, and commenced to weep a little; whereat Mc-
Namara realized she had been really frightened. She
shook his hand warmly, thanked him and departed.

For several minutes McNamara sat thinking, a little
smile, faintly tender, illuminating his rugged countenance. So Lanny had kissed Sapphire Susie and given
her a hundred dollars and begged her to be a good girl
in the future. What a rare good sport Lanny was! And
how good God has been to all concerned! In their pur-
suit of Nance, Flynn and Angelloti had followed such
a hot trail they had forgotten Sapphire Susie was a pal
of Nance's, but when the trail grew cold, they had remembered her.

That Flynn was a marvel, and McNamara sighed to
think the fellow could not be promoted instantly. In
all probability he had not at first connected Nance
Belden with the glory of Susie's sapphires. Undoubtedly
he had jumped to the conclusion that the girl had been
up to her old trick of blackmailing some wealthy and
socially prominent masculine jackass. So he had looked
up her record in the police files. Here he had discovered
something that must have convinced him of Susie's
total innocence of sapphires during her trial; certainly
she had not carried them to San Quentin with her, and
the obvious conclusion was that she had pawned them
to raise money to pay her attorney. In the hope of discovering the identity of Susie's latest victim (who, he
assumed, had redeemed them for her) Flynn had thereupon made a round of the pawn-shops and located the

one from which the jewels had lately been redeemed; from the pawnbroker he had got a description of the one who had redeemed them. Any pawnbroker would be unlikely to forget Nance Belden's'nose!

McNamara shuddered. If Nance should visit Sapphire Susie now, she would undoubtedly walk straight into the arms of the waiting Flynn or Angelloti.

Well, Nance Belden had stolen a dozen pairs of silk hose, but apparently Penelope Gatlin paid her debts. The chief wondered if he had loaned Nance Belden or Penelope Gatlin two hundred dollars, for of course they were two separate and distinct personalities inhabiting the same body. If Nance Belden had accepted the loan, then McNamara could kiss the money good-by.

If, on the other hand, Penelope Gatlin had accepted it, then, some day, from Penelope he would get it back. Well, he could trace her progress through the world by the drafts she would cash. Her bank in San José would give him that information.

He took down the telephone and called the bank. Yes, a draft had just come in, drawn for four hundred and thirty-five dollars in favor of the French Line, dated three days previously at New York. It had come across the continent by air mail. McNamara thanked the president of the bank and called up the French Line's San Francisco office. After some difficulty he discovered that four hundred and thirty-five dollars was payment of one first-cabin passage to Havre and that the Ile de France had sailed from New York during the last three days.

Instantly Dan McNamara shot a straight telegram to police headquarters in New York requesting that the passenger list of the Ile de France be checked to see whether Nance Belden and Penelope Gatlin had taken passage on her. Four hours later he received a reply to the effect that Nance Belden was not aboard but that Penelope Gatlin was.

"Nothing is lost if you know where it is," McNamara decided happily, and sent a cable to the prefect of police at Havre, requesting him to pick up Penelope Gatlin on her arrival at that port, shadow her and report by cable, collect, the girl's destination, the names and addresses of those who should meet her and any other information that would aid in keeping track of the girl.

The following day Dan McNamara sent for Detective-Sergeants Flynn and Angelloti. As they ranged themselves, more or less at attention, in front of his desk, the chief leaned back in his chair and bent upon the pair a long, severe and penetrating look. They grew a little fidgety before he spoke.

"Well, boys, how are your private affairs prospering?"

Both shrugged, unwilling to be definite about anything.

"They are unprosperous," the chief challenged, "so I have called you in to express the hope that you are now quite willing to abandon your private practice and return to work for the city and county of San Francisco. You draw salary from the tax-payers, you know. I may have been mistaken, Angelloti, but I thought I saw you out in Mission recently when you were supposed to be working on that racketeer killing over in North Beach. However, I'll overlook that on the assumption that you permitted yourself to be led astray by Flynn. Flynn, you lay off Sapphire Susie until that enterprising young woman does something you can pin on her. Then bring her in."

"She's done something and I'll pin it on her yet," Flynn growled, "and you know what it is." Flynn, being Irish, was unwilling that his chief should regard him as deficient in intelligence and enterprise.

"We understand each other thoroughly, Flynn. You've been after that Belden girl and you've made a mess of it." He opened his desk drawer and drew out two envelopes. One was addressed to Flynn and the other to Angelloti and both envelopes bore the return address of a prominent New York hotel, but were neither stamped nor postmarked. "These two envelopes came in a large envelope addressed to me," McNamara explained. "They're sealed!" He handed each detective his letter and watched as they opened them and drew forth typewritten letters and two hundred and fifty dollars in bills. Flynn's letter was, undoubtedly, a copy of Angelloti's.

Flynn perused his letter and handed it to the chief, who read:

Dear Mr. Flynn:

You poor dear, you have worked so hard and so intelligently and in such dreadfully hard luck that my heart goes out to you. You were working for the reward, of course—no doubt because you needed the money. You and Mr. Angelloti would have had to divide two hundred and fifty dollars had you recaptured me, but just to prove I'm a sport and not holding any mean little grudge, I'm sending you each two hundred and fifty dollars. Please be good and try to forget all the unpleasant incidents. You will never get me now, so do give up your attempts, like good boys.

The letter was unsigned.

"How much did you get, Angelloti?" McNamara queried softly.

"Two fifty, chief."

"Santa Claus has been good to you two, hasn't he? Well, are you both willing to go back to your regular jobs now?"

Flynn threw the money on the chief's desk. "We swore an oath—" he began, but McNamara cut him short.

"So have I!" he reminded Flynn fiercely. "Now look here, Pat. I've had enough of your shenanigans. Your people came from Belfast, and the wind from Belfast spoils my people's spuds." He glowered at Angelloti. "And I'm not so fond of macaroni, either."

"We know every move you've made in this case," Flynn shouted.

"And I knew every move you were going to make before you made it. That's why I'm chief of police while you two are still detective-sergeants. Take your money and get out, or leave it with me and get out anyhow."

Angelloti tucked his present in his pocket, "Come on, Flynn," he urged.

"I can't be called off for money," Flynn persisted stubbornly.

Dan McNamara swept the money on his desk into the drawer. "The widows and orphans of the Policeman's Benevolent and Protective Association will be glad to get this two hundred and fifty, Flynn. On your way—you and your oath. Out!"

Flynn sighed deeply and went out. Fifteen minutes later he came back and said humbly: "Chief, I've changed my mind."

Alas! McNamara was Irish, too, hence contrary and on occasion spiteful. He glanced at the clock. "You're fifteen minutes late, so I'll fine you two hundred and fifty dollars for tardiness and impudence and disloyalty and housebreaking. And if you come into my office again before I send for you, I'll take you apart to see if it's true that the son of an Orangeman has black spots on his heart and white spots on his liver."

"I'll get you for this, McNamara!"

"I don't think so. My advice to you, Pat Flynn, would be to quit monkeying with T.N.T. I've known detective-sergeants to be taken for a ride."

"Threatening me, eh?"

"Not at all. I wouldn't harm a hair of your red head—and by the way, red hair in the Irish is a sign that they breed back to the Danes and Swedes that invaded Ireland in the ninth century. A pure-bred Irishman would know enough to lay off a girl with powerful and implacable friends. I'm smart enough—and I'm not getting a cent for it, either. All you were after was a hundred and twenty-five dollars—half the state reward for recapturing that girl—and when she sends you double that you're not sport enough to meet her half-way. What's your grouch?"

"I took an oath," Flynn mumbled stubbornly.

"You should have taken a physic?"

"Well, I did take an emetic. Chief, I'll never forgive you those tear and stink bombs. They was awful. You let that girl and that nurse, Lanning, make monkeys of me an' Angelloti. You hurt our feelings an' wrecked our professional pride."

"Well, you shadowed my house and entered it unlawfully."

"We never did."

"You lie. Didn't I hang a mouse on Angelloti's left eye when I caught him watching my house? I could have captured him if I had wanted him, but I didn't, so I just put my mark on him so I'd know when I saw him again I hadn't made any mistake."

"I found a lip-stick and a compact—"

"Belonged to the nurse I had looking after a sick

friend of mine that was stopping with me," the chief lied glibly.

But Flynn only grinned ferociously and shook his red head. "I found stained bandages, too."

"Well, the pot can't get nowhere by calling the kettle black," McNamara decided. "Clear out!"

"Give me the money and I'll lay off," Flynn pleaded.

But Dan McNamara shook his head. "I know your kind, Pat. They hold grudges and shoot from behind hedges and double-cross their own mothers. There's no sense wasting good money on you because you won't stay bought. Clear out, I tell you."

So Flynn cleared out, carrying with him infinitely more respect for his chief than he had heretofore entertained. He even managed a little grin as he reflected how thoroughly McNamara had measured him. Well, he'd lost—but some day he would win. He was patient. He could wait. And he never forgot names or faces. Some day he'd collect heavy interest on that two hundred and fifty dollars.

CHAPTER TWELVE

THE last patient had left Stephen Burt's office for the day and the ever-watchful Lanny had locked the office door against a possible late-comer.

"Tired, Stevie?" she queried anxiously as she watched him load his pipe and swing his long legs up on his desk.

"No, of course not," he replied abruptly. "What have I done to be tired?"

"Well, you had another session with that terrible Mrs. Merton."

"She doesn't weary me any more. She doesn't even bore me. She merely excites my sympathy. The poor wretch has become a sun-worshiper—a chaotic mixture of theology and actinic rays. Still sleepless, of course, and still bothered about her poor devil of a husband. She's had detectives on his trail for a month. They've cost her ten dollars a day each and they haven't discovered anything to Merton's discredit."

"It's about time for Mrs. Merton to commence hearing voices of sorts," Lanny commented dryly. "Highball, Stevie?"

"Yes, thank you, Lanny—if you'll spare me the unutterable depravity of drinking alone. I love this little let-down of half an hour after the heat and the burdens of the day," he added, and deluged Lanny with his sunny smile. "Yes, Mrs. Merton is hearing voices. Her first husband, who is dead, keeps whispering through space to her. He's trying to tell her how sorry he is that he treated her so cruelly. I understand he made a dirty will."

"He would—if he had any common sense." Lanny pulled out the telephone plug to insure her beloved additional privacy. "What a beaten poor devil Merton is! He hasn't the courage of a mouse."

"What can he do, Lanny? His wife is unbalanced, but if he swears out a warrant, charging her with insanity, she'll snap out of her lunacy. It's a mighty serious thing to deprive a human being of her liberty. Boards of alienists are forever disagreeing on what constitutes insanity, psychoses, neuroses, and what have we. Mrs. Merton isn't sufficiently insane to be incarcerated. In many respects she's a mighty bright woman. And she's a beautiful woman, well-to-do, respectable; Merton couldn't get to first base on an insanity warrant.

"Then why doesn't he divorce her on grounds of mental cruelty?"

"The man's chivalrous and profoundly sympathetic. He cannot bear the thought of that irresponsible creature thrown on her own resources. Besides, he hasn't any witnesses to prove a charge of mental cruelty. And he can't run away from her because he has a thriving business he may not abandon."

"If I were Merton I'd sell my business and go so far from that nutty woman a post-card couldn't reach me," said Lanny.

"I told her again today not to come to my office any more; that I could do nothing for her; that she was a nuisance—and to try some other doctor. She went out in a rage."

"She'll be back, Stevie."

"Do not send the poor devil any more bills. It was ethical to bill him for her visits while I was treating her, but I told him a month ago I could do nothing for her. And I told her today I wasn't going to make him any further charges and for that reason she must not impose on my time and good nature. Instantly she said: 'Well, that's just another evidence of my husband's lack of sympathy. He has conspired with you to do this, because he's too stingy to pay my bills.'"

"The next time she comes I'm not going to let her in to see you, dearie," Lanny decided.

"You'll have a battle on your hands if you adhere to that decision, Lanny."

"I'm no clinging vine, Stevie. Now who do you suppose that is knocking? Your office hours are plainly printed on the door."

"Oh, Lanny, don't be so hard-boiled. Let the patient in."

"Who's there?" Lanny shouted angrily.

"Oh! So it's you, is it? I knew you were there," the voice of Dan McNamara boomed back at her.

Lanny unlocked the door and said smilingly: "Lucky for you you're not a nut, Dan McNamara. Welcome. Stevie and I are just pinning one on."

"I'll join you, if that's the case." McNamara proffered his huge hand, that resembled nothing so much in life as a bunch of bananas. "Howdy, medico." He planted himself in the visitor's chair.

"You have news of Nance Belden," Stephen challenged.

"Gobs of it, doctor."

Lanny entered with a highball. "I had a letter from Nance yesterday, Dan," she announced. "She's in Paris. Can you beat that?"

"I can," McNamara replied coolly. "She's got an apartment at twenty-seven rue-St. Honoré, with a cook named Laurette Manitan and a maid named Fleurette Dejean and a chauffeur named Jean Gagneau, who drives her around in a Citroen car. And she's having her picture painted by an American artist."

"She's written you, too, then?"

"Divil a line. I have my information from the prefect of police of Paris. You don't suppose I was going to let the poor nut escape from me entirely, do you?"

"Dan, you're marvelous, positively uncanny!"

"What's more, Lanny, she's living with her normal personality."

"How do you know?"

"She registered with the police, as required by law, under her real name of Penelope Gatlin."

"You know that?"

"I've known it since the day after her escape from San Quentin." And McNamara proceeded to relate the tale he had previously related to Stephen, who, for reasons best known to himself, had neglected to retail it to Lanny. The latter's amazement found characteristic expression. "Well, if this isn't a hell of a tale, Dan!"

"Does it beat your news, Lanny?"

"Beats it a mile, although while she was at my house she told me as much about herself as she could remember. There seemed to be a hiatus for the past two years."

"This morning," McNamara continued, "the president of the Security Trust Company telephoned me that the girl's mother had called him up to ask if Penelope had been cashing any checks lately. The banker gathered that the mother has a notion her daughter's dead, and was just checking up to prove her case. She doesn't like the idea of having to wait seven years to have the girl declared officially dead before she can lay claim to Penelope's estate."

"Did you find out the name of her mother?" Stephen asked.

"I did. The first time I interviewed that bank president he couldn't remember it—she's married again, you understand—but she introduced herself over the telephone this morning and gave her address. Naturally she didn't get any information out of the banker. He's

on to her, and it was none of her business whether
Penelope has been cashing checks or not. A bank pro-
tects the secrets of its depositors until subpœnaed to
tell them in court."

"Get the girl's case record, Lanny," Stephen commanded, and Lanny produced it from the files. Stephen
took up his fountain pen. "What is her mother's name,
chief?"

"Mrs. Rudolph Merton."

"Ow-w-w-w!"

Lanny's lamentation brought Dan McNamara up
with a jerk. "You got me skinned on the low-down
after all," he charged.

"She's a patient of Stevie's," Lanny yelled. "She's
such a nut the squirrels chase her."

Stephen finished writing and laid down his pen.
"I told you, Lanny, that Mrs. Merton wasn't insane
enough to be confined. She's not so insane she doesn't
reason pretty coherently in the matter of her daughter's estate. She knows her legal rights as a mother."

"Guess I've got Lanny's news beaten after all,
Stephen. This Mrs. Rudolph Merton isn't the girl's
mother. She's her foster-mother."

"Hooray! Hooray! Hooray!" cried Lanny. "How do
you know this? Did the banker tell you?"

"No. I dug the information up myself."

"Why? How?"

"Why? Because you gave up hope for the girl when
I told you her mother was a devil on wheels and a re-

ligious fanatic. You felt there was a neurotic streak in
Nance, inherited from her mother. I wanted to make
certain about that and I wanted to investigate the girl's
fortune. So yesterday I had a copy of the will and a
copy of the appraisal of the estate made at the court
house in San José and sent up to me. Gatlin stated in
the will that he left all of his estate to his beloved
adopted daughter, Penelope Gatlin. At the time of his
death his estate was worth practically half a million
dollars and has since doubled in value. Nance Belden is
a lost heiress."

"Not wholly lost," Stephen reminded him. "There
are times when she remembers who she is and that she
has money in the Security Trust Company of San
José."

"She doesn't know anything about her mother,"
Lanny declared. "I asked her, but she could tell me
nothing. And she was Penelope Gatlin when I asked
her."

"There is a reason for that." Dr. Burt's scientific
mind was already racing along this new trail. "Penelope has had a wretched childhood; she knew nothing
but unhappiness up to the time she received the shock
that threw her mental gears out of mesh. Long-con-
tinued unhappiness and rebellious thoughts laid the seed
for her present condition; some profound shock caused
the seed to germinate. She hated her mother with a
terrible hatred. Feared her, probably. For a reason
which we shall one day uncover, she made up her mind

to forget her mother, since only in forgetfulness could she find peace of mind. And the will to forget was so strong that she succeeded beyond her expectations."

"Not only did she forget her mother, but her entire past life as well, for of course, while she did not realize it at the time, her vow to forget included every incident of her life with which her mother was connected. She ran away from her mother; she wanted to disappear, to be free forever of her mother's hateful dominance and presence. Well, she disappeared, and she'll never find her way back until she acquires sufficient courage to face the old issues again, surmount them and defeat them. She will get well when she makes up her mind to remember the life she resolved to forget."

"But is that possible?" McNamara asked, all attention.

"Quite. She will have to have assistance and the sort of treatment I think I can give her, and she must have assurance that never again will she be subjected to the old unhappiness. Even though I have had a very superficial opportunity to study the girl, I realize that her nature is one that craves love and understanding. She responds to affection as a wilted flower responds to water. Poor waif! She yearned for love and believed she would never attain it because she was ugly and repulsive. Of course she magnified the situation. Dan, can't you understand why a soul that had never known anything for a decade save torture should disintegrate under the blows that Fate was raining upon it?"

The chief nodded. "I suppose seventy per cent of the queer fish that come to my net never had a Chinaman's chance of happiness, Steve."

"By the way," asked Stephen, "I wonder if Penelope was a love child. Have you looked up her parentage, Dan?"

"I haven't. But if this Mrs. Merton is a patient of yours, can't you ask her about the girl?"

"I suppose I could. But if either of her parents was a lunatic, or if lunacy ran in the family of her father or mother, I'm not going to bother with Penelope."

"If you decide to take her on, we'll have to get her back into this city," McNamara mourned, "and Flynn will pick her up."

"We'll fix her nose first," Lanny assured him.

McNamara beamed upon her. "Her criminal photographs and Bertillon measurements are gone to glory, Lanny. I've seen to that."

"Dan McNamara, you're a darling. Have another drink?"

"Since you insist," he answered patiently. "What did Penelope have to say in her letter to you?"

"Not a great deal," Lanny answered. "She said, among other things, that after leaving my house she found she had two hundred dollars and assumed that I had given it to her. So she returned it."

"Give me that two hundred, Lanny. Stephen, our little thief is honest."

"She was Penelope Gatlin until just before you gave

her that money, Dan," said Lanny. "As Nance Belden she would remember you gave her two hundred dollars, but as Penelope Gatlin, later, she couldn't remember who gave it to her. She could only guess."

"Get over to Paris as quick as you can," McNamara commanded, "or she'll be stealing the Eiffel Tower."

"Stephen can't spare me," Lanny protested.

"Stephen *can* spare you," her employer decided.

"But, Stevie dear—"

"But me no buts. You have a trip coming to you. I'm a rich man because you've taken entire charge of my business and the investment of my fees. This is my treat, Lanny."

"It's got to be," McNamara urged. "Nance fled the town with a letter of credit for ten thousand, but she'll go through that like a weasel through a rat hole, and when it's gone she can't get any more for six months. So she'll help herself to whatever she thinks she needs. Take a bank-roll with you, Lanny, and when you get there take charge of Penelope and her funds."

"And have her nose done over while you're there. You're the nurse for that job," Stephen urged.

"How do you know Penelope will bankrupt herself, Dan?"

"Because she's having her picture painted by an expensive artist, for one thing—"

"There's another hitch," said Lanny. "The girl evidently got a passport in New York—"

"Not in New York. In San Francisco," McNamara

interrupted. "I've looked up the record. Ella Cates, the wife of one of the men that rescued her from the bay, was her witness that she was a citizen of the United States. Not having any birth certificate, she had to have a witness."

"Well, will a strange photograph on her passport get her back into the United States?"

"She can go to the American consul in Paris, and present proof that she's the same woman with a different nose. That's easily fixed," Stephen declared.

"She'll do nothing of the sort." McNamara was very emphatic. "When her trail is lost it will be lost forever. Lanny, when you have that new nose built for the girl and it's a perfect job with no scars showing, have half a dozen new passport photographs of her taken, and send them and her passport to me. The seal of the United States of America is on the passport and covers a part of the photograph. I know a man that'll make me a seal that would fool the American eagle himself. We'll fit it down over the old seal and stamp the new photograph. Then I'll send it back to you—and may God have mercy on my soul, for you can blackmail me for that the longest day I live."

This was too much. Lanny put her arms around him and kissed him on each cheek.

"And that's a seal that'll get by, too." McNamara was much embarrassed. Lanny was, too—after she had had about three seconds to think it over—so she took a hasty departure.

The two men stared after her, admiration in their eyes. "A damned fine woman, that. None finer," said McNamara.

"Why don't you marry her?" The suggestion popped out of Dr. Burt as suddenly as it had occurred to him.

McNamara smoothed back his rebellious pompadour. "Now, there's an idea," he mumbled dazedly.

"The idea has merit. Mull it over, Mac."

"How long have you been mulling it over?"

"Subconsciously, since you entered the office. I caught a gleam in Lanny's eyes—and when she kissed you, the subconscious crystallized into the conscious."

"I'll think it over." McNamara was still dazed. "But you couldn't very well get along without her, could you? And how do you know she'll have me?"

"You'll not think it over, Mac. You'll make up your mind now. And I can get along without her, although the going will be pretty skiddy. But of course she'll marry you if you ask her. Lanny never proffers her friendships or her loves on the half-shell. Dan, she's lonely. Somehow, she missed out on life. She was meant for a fine wife and mother. She's over forty, but—there's still time, my boy, still time."

"Not if she goes to Paris." McNamara's face had lengthened. "She'll be gone six months at least."

"I've heard of police chiefs securing a leave of absence for six months."

"I have a good record," McNamara admitted.

"Well, shake a leg."

"I couldn't take a six months' honeymoon to Paris, lad. I've saved eight thousand dollars—"

"What? You a chief of police and only worth eight thousand dollars? You amaze me."

"God help me, boy, I'm honest."

Stephen roared his merriment. "Why, you great jackass, I know that. I wouldn't let every man have Lanny, you understand. I know her worth. But don't you worry about money. I was born without the acquisitive sense, without respect for material values. But Lanny is a business woman. She's managed me, and that includes my finances. She knows some stock and bond broker who appears to be not only a brilliant financier but a very honest, decent man, and a good friend of Lanny's. She follows his advice in my investments. I don't know what she's won and I don't know what she's lost, but I do know I'm loaded up with good dividend-paying stocks that have appreciated tremendously in value.

"Lanny made me, Dan. I'm here to tell you, Dan McNamara, that if Lanny was ten years younger I wouldn't let you have her. I'd marry her myself. I owe Lanny much more than I ever can repay; she shall have the best of it while I live, and I have made ample provision for her in my will." He paused a moment while he gazed meaningly upon the chief. "You know, Dan, I could be a mighty good friend to the man who would be good to Lanny."

"I'll consider the proposition," the cautious Celt replied, "although I'd rather be a bachelor than a disappointed lover—at my age. I'll have to be sure of my ground."

"Tell you what to do, Mac," Stephen advised. "Send her a nice photograph of yourself—in uniform and on a prancing horse at the head of a parade. If she puts it in a silver frame you may proceed with confidence."

"How will I know, my boy?"

"Take a look—see, you idiot. If it's in a silver frame on the dressing-table in her bedroom, it'll be a cinch."

"How'll I get into her bedroom, you blockhead?"

"I'll steal her latch-key out of her purse, send it out, and have a duplicate key made in half an hour. Then, while she's at the office, you can make your investigation."

McNamara rose and held out his hand. " 'Tis a pity, Stephen, my boy, you aren't in my detective bureau. Good night and God bless you."

As the reader has doubtless already suspected, Dan McNamara was one who, without the aid of a twelve-power glass, could see a hole in a ladder. The annual inspection and parade of the police force was but a week distant, and during that week McNamara lived entirely on orange juice and spent his nights in a Turkish bath, with a deal of massaging night and morning. As a result he dropped eight pounds off his northern elevation. Very erect and martial he sat a milk-white charger at the head of a platoon of mounted police, while a photographer took several exposures of him.

When the prints were delivered to him he sent them all to Lanny with a note saying:

"Now that we are both in the same crooked conspiracy I thought you might be interested in having the latest photo of the biggest crook of them all."

The following day Stephen Burt sent him a key, sans comment, and the following afternoon McNamara let himself into Lanny's house and discovered one of the photos on her dressing-table—and in a gold frame! Another print in a silver frame appeared on top of the piano in her drawing-room.

"Holy Moses!" he soliloquized. "I'm in for it now! God help me, there's no escape!"

Upon his return to his office he found in his mail a photograph of Lanny, endorsed: "To dear old Dan—from his partner in crime—Lanny." While he was gazing upon it and telling himself how little justice the portrait did the beloved subject, Stephen telephoned, demanding, rather excitedly, that he come to the office immediately.

Upon his arrival Lanny, in tears, ushered him in to Stephen. "I've just had another visit from Mrs. Rudolph Merton, Dan," the latter began in his quick, incisive manner. "It seems that after two years of inactivity, during which time she had elected to believe Penelope Gatlin dead, she has developed a crazy notion to prove it. She wants to get Penelope's fortune, and as you suspected, she just can't wait seven years to have the girl declared officially dead. Of course, you and I

know she isn't dead, but we'll swim a bloody river before we'll tell her. If she found her she'd undo all the
good work I hope to accomplish."

"You questioned her about her daughter, did you?"

"Yes, but she doesn't know it. I hypnotized her first
and spent an hour questioning her. We psychiatrists
employ hypnotism to a considerable extent, particularly in cases of amnesia, and I've become rather adroit
at it—that is, when the patient permits it. Well, I questioned her, and it appears that this morning she visited
your captain of detectives and asked him to throw out
a drag-net to locate Penelope Gatlin. She brought him
some snapshots of the girl—told him her real name—
all about her money in the trust fund of the Security
Trust Company of San José—their life together abroad
—the girl's habits and peculiarities—everything. When
I'd discovered enough to put Lanny in tears and scare
us both out of a year's growth, I awakened Mrs. Merton and sent her away happy, but with this command
firmly planted in her subconscious mind—she must not
think of the name Penelope Gatlin. I warned her during
the hypnotic state that that name was associated with
death and misery; I commanded her never to mention
that name again; I assured her she couldn't even think
of it if she wanted to. Dan, it worked! When I awakened her I asked her if she had an adopted daughter.
She replied, surprised, that she had. I then asked her
the name of this adopted daughter—and a look of
terror came over her face. For the life of her she

couldn't think of the name and begged me not to mention it if I knew it."

"It's a pity you didn't think of doing that before she went to the detective bureau with her information," McNamara cried, and called up the president of the Security Trust Company on Stephen's telephone.

"The captain of detectives has put Flynn and Angelloti on the case," he announced drearily when he had hung up, "and Flynn has already been to the bank, making inquiries. When he presented his credentials, the cashier, in the absence of the president, showed him everything. Flynn now knows the girl bought a letter of credit for ten thousand dollars, and he's smart enough to realize that she planned to leave the country. He'll work the passport office and Angelloti will scout around among the people who saw Penelope frequently while she was in the city prison awaiting trial. He'll show those snapshots to the judge, to the district attorney, to the turnkey and jailer, to the matron at San Quentin. He'll identify Penelope Gatlin as Nance Belden as sure as death and taxes; he and Flynn will trace her to Paris as readily as I did, and the French government will be notified that Penelope is an escaped convict. They will immediately deport her and cable the chief of detectives the name of her boat. Flynn will meet her at the dock."

"But can't you do anything about it, Dan?" Lanny pleaded.

"Nothing! Flynn and Angelloti are on the trail offi-

cially now, and all I can do, if the news comes down to
me from the upper office, is to cheer them on." He
stared at Lanny and Stephen tragically and said with
heavy·finality: "I'm out of the picture now and can
do nothing but advise you. Send two cables—one to
Nance Belden in Paris and the other to Penelope Gatlin at the same address. Say: 'Come at once—Lanny
dying—cable name vessel on which leaving,' and sign
your cable 'Steve.' If she can get to New York before
Flynn gets there, we'll have a fighting chance."

"I'll meet her at the dock," Stephen decided. "I'm
due in New York for a convention next week."

"You'll do nothing of the sort. You and Lanny will
keep out of this. I'll send that sick convict at my house.
My mother's coming home and I have to get rid of
him." He shuddered and grimaced in his distress. "I
could handle the wop with money, but that low, red-
headed Orange scoundrel, Pat Flynn, has sworn an
oath! And because I've made a monkey out of him he'll
keep it. He'd rather make a monkey out of me now
than acquire great riches—and if I'm broke, most
likely the captain of detectives will step into my shoes,
and Flynn will stand a good chance of becoming captain of detectives. Oh, murderation, Lanny darling,
have you a little whisky in the house? I'm faint, so I
am."

"You're suffering from heart trouble, you egg,"
Lanny cried savagely. "Yes! A weak heart, a soft
heart, a human heart."

"Cut out the shenanigans and send that cable," he roared.

"Yes, get busy, Lanny," Stephen urged gently. "The bird of time has but a little way to flutter—and the wretched fowl is on the wing."

After Dan McNamara had left his office, Dr. Stephen Burt sat and smoked tranquilly and gazed with mild disapproval upon Lanny, who stood it for about a minute and then said petulantly:

"Well, out with it. Don't you sulk with me, Stevie."

"Unlike you and Dan McNamara I dislike having the peaceful tenor of my life disturbed. Unlike Dan, who is all Irish, and you, who are half Irish, intrigue does not appeal to me."

"This particular intrigue is myrrh and incense to me, Stevie."

"I know it. You and Dan love a fight for its own sweet sake, but I do not. I have a particular aversion to grand jury indictments, and that is a possibility you and your boy friend have let me in for."

"Fiddlesticks!"

"Lanny, I'll be angry with you in a minute. Now, listen to me and whatever you do, do not talk back. I can't bear insubordination. Dan McNamara has run out on us—I mean you. He's through. Enough is enough, and he is a wise man who knows when he has had sufficient. Dan's rattled—frightened for the first time. If he hadn't been, he'd never have ordered the sending of such a fool cablegram."

"Dan McNamara knows his way about," Lanny defended. "He's more than nine years old."

"So do I. Lanny, it will be highly dangerous to send that cablegram. How is she to know it isn't a false message to decoy her back to San Quentin? If she receives it while she's Penelope Gatlin, she is extremely liable to cable for confirmation before acting on it. That would mean a delay of not less than twenty-four hours, and in the interim the Paris police will have nabbed her. On the other hand, if she is Nance Belden when she receives it, she will leave Paris openly—leave a trail behind her that any fool may follow—and walk right into the hands of the New York police. They'll pick her up at quarantine. I'm not much of a detective, but tonight I'm a much better one than that McNamara idiot."

"He's not an idiot. He's one of the finest men I have ever known."

"No good in a pinch." Stephen waved her protests aside. "Keep quiet," he ordered severely. "You ditch my train of thought."

He drew a sheet of paper toward him and commenced writing, while Lanny glowered at him. There were occasions when she fairly ached to box his ears, and this was one of them. Presently he sat up and read:

"Grave danger stop beat it some other country traveling by motor stop upon arrival cable address stop if need funds will cable them stop leave your Paris establishment a going concern stop go out for a ten

minute walk and disappear saying nothing to anybody
stop unless these instructions followed you leave trail
for your persecutors to follow. Mac."

He looked up at Lanny. "How do those instructions strike you?"

"The instructions are fine, but why commit forgery
by signing Dan's name to the cablegram. If the original is ever traced—"

"I have signed it Mac, not McNamara, and the
world is quite filled with Mac's and O's. We'll alibi
Daniel. When he has reached his office telephone him
what we're doing and for him to do something that
will prove in any court he was in his office when I filled
this cablegram."

Lanny relented. "You might make a detective at
that."

Twenty minutes later Dan McNamara was listening
to Lanny reading Stephen's cablegram over his private
line. "Excellent," was his sole comment, "but print it
in block letters. Even a typewriter can betray one as
well as one's handwriting. When Steve files this telegram have him pay with a five-hundred-dollar bill
and have him wear large black goggles and the rim of
his hat pulled down all the way round. That cablegram
will excite the curiosity of the girl who receives it for
transmission. She'll think one crook is cabling another,
so she'll look Stephen over very carefully and she'll
remember the five-hundred-dollar bill. If she's asked
what sort of man filed it her description of the sender,
plus my own perfect alibi, will put me in the clear."

"How are we to manage after she has eluded the Paris police?"

McNamara sighed gustily. "Flynn will be in touch with her bank in San José, and every time she cashes a draft on her letter of credit and that draft comes home to roost, Flynn will have a line on her address. He can chase her clear around the world and land her in the long run, unless she goes to Timbuktu, where, I believe, nobody gives a hoot what anybody has done elsewhere, provided they behave themselves in Timbuktu."

"You're no help," Lanny snapped, and hung up. She repeated Dan's instructions to Stephen, who nodded his agreement, and half an hour later, from the cable company's main office he dispatched the cablegram.

He was now undecided whether Penelope Gatlin had developed into a common nuisance, an interesting study in that most fascinating and mysterious field, the human mind, or a duty that might not be shirked. She appeared destined to bob up like an importunate creditor, bringing with her a new element of interest, just as he was about to congratulate himself on forgetting her. Against the police power of the state and the nation, the State Department, the Paris police, and the French government, he, Lanny, and Dan McNamara were arrayed in a battle to a finish; and a pretty kettle of fish they would all be in should their activities be proved. Of course the interest of the chief

and Lanny was warmly human; they wanted to win the
fight and were not at all particular as to how they
won it. On the other hand, Stephen's interest was coldly
scientific, and he felt that he had inflicted upon his
conservatism and intelligence a needless affront when
he permitted himself to be swept into this intrigue now
so pregnant of disaster.

With McNamara definitely out of the fight, Stephen
felt lonely and apprehensive, for he knew the situation was in the laps of the gods. If Penelope Gatlin
should walk down the gangplank into the waiting arms
of P. Flynn, it was more than probable she would protect her friends by obstinately refusing to yield to the
cajoleries of the astute Flynn. On the other hand,
should Nance Belden walk down that gangplank, nobody knew better than Stephen that she would be out
of control and anything might happen, and probably
would.

He wondered why the girl had fled to Paris, in the
face of Dan McNamara's instructions to flee to Lower
California, to enter which no passport is required. So
when Lanny came to work next day he asked her to
solve this conundrum.

"Oh, that's no mystery, Stevie. I had brought home
from the office, intending to show it to Dan, a copy of
the Journal of the American Medical Association, with
an article in it by Dr. Jules Arnaud, the celebrated
plastic surgeon of Paris. It was a very interesting
article, descriptive of his technique, and profusely illus-

trated with before-and-after pictures. He accomplished miracles on soldiers who had their chins and noses shot away in battle. I showed the article to Penelope, and she read it with great interest. She went to Paris to consult this French plastic surgeon and also to have samples of her new nose drawn by a competent artist."

"So that's why the Paris police informed Dan she was having her portrait done by an American artist, eh? Well, even if she has a psychoneurosis she can use her head a little. I suppose it will be her luck to be in a hospital undergoing the operation when the Paris police receive word to gather her in and deport her."

"I'm afraid she's balled everything up, Stephen. Flynn will have the number of her passport, and Dan will have no time to fix a new passport photograph onto it. They'll not trust to the photo to identify her if she tries to land. They'll check up on the passport number also."

"Will you never cease discussing this miserable business, Lanny?" Stephen burst out irritably. "If it hadn't been for you we wouldn't be in this wretched predicament. Stop it—and let's try to make a living out of this nut shop today."

CHAPTER THIRTEEN

WHEN the captain of detectives called in Detective-Sergeant P. Flynn and related to him the tale told to him by Mrs. Rudolph Merton, Flynn gave no sign of being particularly interested. Carefully and methodically he arrayed in his mind the facts as stated, and when he left the presence of his superior all he knew was that he was to strive to recover a lost heiress, by name Penelope Gatlin, and that Penelope Gatlin had a ruined nose that should make her readily recognizable anywhere.

After dinner that night Flynn retired early and awakened about five o'clock the following morning, after nine hours of refreshing slumber. Experience had indicated to him that this was the time he could do his best thinking. His mind was, for the moment, free of disturbance, it was rested, refreshed. So, quite automatically, he proceeded to ponder the case of Penelope Gatlin of the saddle nose, the heiress who had so mysteriously dropped from view two years before. "I seem to be getting my fill of girls with saddle noses who disappear mysteriously," he decided lazily—and instantly something clicked in his brain and he knew he was on the trail of Nance Belden again. An heiress, eh? McNamara had hinted at powerful influences back of Nance Belden, and they certainly must have had money to throw away in order to have hired the expert help she had had in her escape from San Quentin.

"McNamara knows who she is," Flynn decided. "He's getting his—in chunks—for helping her. By God! I'll bet it's the same girl."

He decided not to take Angelloti into his confidence, for Angelloti wasn't entitled to it. For and in consideration of the sum of two hundred and fifty dollars paid to him, Angelloti had agreed to abandon his interest in Nance Belden, whereas P. Flynn, the resolute, the indomitable, had scorned to quit. Well, he would pick up the trail again alone, and when he had Nance Belden or Penelope Gatlin on his hook he would play her for a sum that would educate all the little Flynns and leave a bit over for the heads of the family in their old age. Send her back to San Quentin again? Nonsense. That would be the act of a fool. She had to pay somebody to keep out of San Quentin and that somebody should be P. Flynn.

He went to San José that day and interviewed the officials of the bank, who, when he flashed his shield, gave him all the information they possessed, including, the fact that the girl had recently purchased a ten-thousand-dollar letter of credit. That, of course, argued travel, and Flynn's heart leaped with joyous anticipation. Dan McNamara had artfully destroyed all the girl's police photographs; but if she had secured a

passport she had left two of her passport photographs
with the passport office, and with the cooperation of
the United States marshal, Flynn knew he could borrow one of these photographs.

It was too late to go to the passport office in the
custom house that day, but Flynn was there when it
opened next morning. His shield was an open sesame
to the man in charge, and two minutes after his arrival
he knew Penelope Gatlin had secured a passport.

Employing identically the same means Dan Mc-
Namara employed, he traced Penelope Gatlin to 27,
rue St.-Honoré, Paris, within three days. But he had
now to prove that Penelope Gatlin and Nance Belden
were one and the same person, so he interviewed the
United States marshal, who secured for him one of
the girl's passport photographs. Armed with this, Flynn
crossed the bay to San Quentin and readily gained
access to the women's quarters.

"Is that Nance Belden?" he asked the matron, and
thrust the photograph under her nose.

"That is Nance Belden," was the reply.

"Absolutely certain?"

"Absolutely."

He showed the photograph to the assistant matron
and from her received the same assurance.

"Now to prove that Nance Belden is the same Penelope Gatlin I'm after," he decided as he recrossed the
bay. He had no doubt that she was, but before proceeding further he must be absolutely certain. So, from

the ferry, he went at once to the home of Mrs. Rudolph Merton, who received him in the drawing-room. She appeared puzzled to understand why he had called, so he stuck the photograph under her nose and asked gruffly:

"Is that your daughter Penelope Gatlin?"

A tremor ran over Mrs. Merton's classically beautiful face. It seemed to Flynn that she was frightened, disturbed. She retreated a few steps from him.

"Well?" he demanded. "You can't expect the police to find your missing daughter if you don't help. Is that Penelope Gatlin?"

"I—I don't know. I have never heard of her before."

"Never heard of her! Why, she's your daughter—your lost daughter!"

"I haven't any daughter."

"Why, you called on the captain of detectives some time back and asked him to find your daughter. What the hell—beg pardon—what do you mean by telling me you've never heard of her?"

"I can't remember. I don't know. Oh, please, please don't ask me. Something terrible will happen. I—I—"

"You refuse to identify this photo as that of Penelope Gatlin?" Flynn was growing irritated.

"I don't know anybody by that name. Oh, I don't want to hear you mention that name again. It frightens me. I—"

In vain Flynn tried all his art to induce Mrs. Merton

to identify the photograph as that of Penelope Gatlin, but equally vain were his attempts to make her admit that the photo was *not* that of Penelope Gatlin. He saw quite clearly that the sound of the name depressed and frightened her, that she appeared to have some sort of inhibition against mentioning it. Finally she had hysterics, and a maid came in and rescued her and asked P. Flynn to leave the house.

Flynn was profoundly irritated. He knew Penelope Gatlin was at 27, rue St.-Honoré, Paris, but he did not know that Nance Belden was! He was morally certain, of course, that they were one and the same person, but he had to be legally certain before starting in motion the legal wheels that would insure her deportation from France as an undesirable alien. Back at Central Office he compared the passport photograph with the substitute photograph Dan McNamara had pasted on Nance Belden's fake police-record card—and knew it for a fake. He knew, too, that Dan McNamara had faked it, and grew correspondingly morose as he reflected that he could never prove that either. He saw very clearly that while the Paris police might be induced to have Penelope Gatlin deported; while the New York police could be induced to pick her up at the gangplank as Nance Belden, she could not be identified as Nance Belden without her prison photographs and Bertillon measurements, in the face of reputable witnesses ready and willing to testify she was Penelope Gatlin.

Suddenly it occurred to Flynn that he had had an

official interview with everybody connected with this mysterious case, with the exception of the fugitive, whom he had never seen, and Dr. Stephen Burt.

"I wonder what sorta bird the doctor is?" Flynn pondered. "He might be a smart man in his profession but no match for me in mine. I think I'll just run up to his office and give him the third degree. No, I'll not do that. I'll call at his house. That cagey Lanning woman would be at his office and spoil everything."

Flynn hadn't the slightest idea what he was going to say to Stephen when he met him; however, he was a resourceful creature who had learned to ask questions in accordance with the effect of a previous question, as reflected in his victim's face. He was capable of a certain suave polish when interviewing a gentleman, and a monstrous ferocity when interviewing a criminal, and had discovered that both modes of operation appeared to work equally well. He decided not to rough Stephen.

At eight o'clock he rang the door-bell at Stephen's house. The butler received his card and bore it upstairs to his master; returning, he begged Flynn to follow him. Stephen was in his upstairs study, a small room with a wood-fire crackling on the hearth and the walls lined with books. He was in dressing-gown and slippers, and as Flynn entered somewhat awkwardly, Stephen rose and advanced upon the detective with hand outstretched. Flynn was uncomfortable under the doctor's roguish smile.

"You're a long time getting around to see me,

sergeant," Stephen charged, and indicated a large, comfortable overstuffed armchair, while the butler relieved Flynn of his derby hat and then proffered him an expensive cigar from an expensive humidor. Flynn took it and bit off and spat the end into the fire.

"I called on you once, doctor, but you didn't know it. That was the night after Nance Belden escaped from San Quentin. Me an' my partner picked you up in front of this house and trailed you to the chief's house, where you fixed up Nance and her wounded pals."

"I've always thought you and the excellent Angelloti didn't make the best of your opportunities in those exciting days," Stephen murmured innocently. "Still, I suppose you were playing with dynamite and had to go slowly."

"We were," said Flynn, "but no more. The chief's one of the biggest-hearted men in the world, but a picnic egg if you rub him the wrong way. So we pussyfooted."

"No fair man could deny the excellence of your pussyfooting. I know all about it."

Flynn chuckled companionably. He liked this young man, and he was more than ever pleased with himself for having decided to take the jovial line of approach. This doctor would be a bad man to try to stop in a dark alley. So Flynn sat back luxuriously, smiling into the flames a prescient, friendly little smile.

"How about a wee doch-an-dorris?" Stephen suggested.

"There's an idea for you, doctor."

Stephen summoned the butler and ordered the drink. Flynn, with great deliberation, produced a wallet and from it extracted Penelope Gatlin's passport photograph. "Know the lady?" he queried, and passed it over.

"I think I do, sergeant."

"Who is she?"

"Is there any reason why I should express an opinion?"

"Not unless you choose to be good-natured," Flynn agreed, without resentment. "I suppose you know you're in Dutch for aiding and abetting an escaped convict—dressing her wounds, knowing who she was and that the police were after her. It is your duty to report to the police when you are called in to treat persons suffering from gunshot or knife wounds."

"Well?"

"Naturally we don't want to make the going hard for a man of your standing," Flynn continued. "It occurred to the chief of detectives you might care to cooperate and save trouble and embarrassment to all concerned."

"My dear sergeant, you would have started the fireworks long ago if you had anything more tangible to proceed upon than suspicion and a moral certainty."

Flynn sipped his highball and considered this answer. "You're being well-paid for shielding this girl, of course. She can afford it. She's worth a million dollars.

I don't blame you a bit, but—I warn you it's dangerous. You're too big a figure in your profession to get into trouble with the police."

"There will be no trouble. Dan McNamara is my friend."

"Well, I'm officially detailed on the case now and Mac is out of it. He daren't show his hand now, and he can't protect you because his first duty is to protect himself."

"Isn't it your duty to protect him, sergeant?"

"I stand between my love and duty, doctor, and duty wins. It might interest you to know that Nance Belden and a lost heiress, Penelope Gatlin, are the same person and that I have the Paris police watching her right now at Number twenty-seven, rue St.-Honoré. As soon as the details can be attended to she'll be deported as an undesirable alien; I will be notified of the name of the steamer she is leaving on, and I'll meet her at the dock. This girl's kinda cuckoo, doc. She'll talk—and if she does—"

He took a pair of bright handcuffs out of his rear pocket and fondled them meaningly. Stephen kicked a slipper up in the air and caught it expertly on his toe as it came down. "Are you quite certain the girl is still at that Paris address?"

"I know it."

"I know she isn't—and the Paris police do not know where she is."

"Do you?"

"No, but if I did I wouldn't tell you."

"Look here." Flynn knew himself to be checkmated. "What's it worth to your snubby-nosed girl friend to have me lay off the case."

"I'll give you twenty dollars in Confederate currency. You were offered real money once and refused it. No 'slips, trails over' in this game, sergeant."

They looked at each other searchingly, then both laughed. "I see there ain't much use pumpin' you, doc," Flynn admitted. "Well, a fellow can't be ruled off for tryin'."

"When were you to see a doctor last?" Stephen shot at him suddenly.

"At the age of twenty-two when I went on the Force. Why?"

"How old are you?"

"Forty-two."

"Well, just to prove I'm friendly I'll give you a quick physical examination while you're here. It may save you a stiff fee later from some other physician. My compliments, sergeant. A man of forty-two who doesn't know his own blood-pressure is a chump. He may be walking in the shadow of death and not know it. You look pretty florid and full-blooded to me. Mind if I give you a quick look-see?"

"A stitch in time saves nine," Flynn admitted. "Go to it."

Stephen tested Flynn's heart-action and lungs with the stethoscope and took his blood-pressure. He directed

Flynn's attention to the recording apparatus. "See that needle, sergeant. It stands at 200. Normal blood-pressure at twenty should be 120, with a two-degree increase for each year thereafter—hence your normal blood-pressure should be about 164. You're up thirty-six points."

"To hell I am," Flynn exclaimed. He was distinctly perturbed. "What does that mean?"

"It means that you have a fairly well-developed case of arteriosclerosis or hardening of the arteries. If this condition continues to progress you will, eventually, reach the stage where you will have to cease all activities. You will be weak and nervous, and any unusual excitement or muscular activity may cause you to blink out like that—" Stephen snapped his fingers. "If you were to be reexamined physically, for promotion, you'd not only be out of the running but you might be retired on pension."

"By Judas, I couldn't afford that. I've got a wife and five children and I've got to support them."

"Nevertheless I would suggest you apply for a six months' leave of absence and have me treat you. I'll not charge you anything. I may be able to bring your blood-pressure down to normal. It's done, you know. You're overweight about twenty-five pounds. How's your eyesight?"

"Grand!" P. Flynn mumbled.

"I doubt it. Sergeant, I'll bet you a hundred dollars you cannot look into this little mirror fifteen minutes without averting your gaze. Want to earn the hundred?"

"I can't afford that much of a bet, doc."

"Well, then, we'll not bet, but just for fun we'll try the experiment, and if you win I'll give you a hundred dollars. Let us say I'm betting with myself. Now, then, lift up your head; settle yourself comfortably in that chair and gaze at the mirror as I hold it."

Stephen produced a small circular mirror from his vest pocket and held it about two feet in front of Flynn and about six inches above the level of the detective's eyes. He took out his watch. "Go," he said. "And remember I'm watching you. If you get through this test successfully there's hope for your arteriosclerosis."

P. Flynn grinned and gazed. In about three minutes the effort of looking fixedly at a bright object somewhat above the normal level of his gaze commenced to oppress him. His eyelids grew heavy; he was sensible of a rapidly growing eye strain. At the end of four minutes Stephen's soothing voice reached him as from a distance.

"You are going to sleep, sergeant—going to sleep. It is an effort for you to keep awake. But do not worry. Fifteen minutes is quite a long test for a man in your condition. Try to stick it out ten minutes."

Flynn blinked, and moisture flooded his eyes. But, despite his dogged courage, his eyelids grew heavier and heavier with the terrific strain of attempting to peer into that little mirror held at that devilish angle.

A tremendous desire to sleep came over him; it was getting more and more difficult to resist it—and presently his eyes closed momentarily. Stephen appeared not to notice this and Flynn opened them again and concentrated doggedly.

"You can't stand it, sergeant. You're going to sleep, I tell you—to sleep. You can't keep your eyes open. You do not want to close them, but you cannot help yourself. See if you can defy me. I command you to close them. Close them, sergeant." His voice grew sympathetic, soft. "You are going to sleep. Do not resist. It is useless. You are going to sleep. Your illness has you. You can't stand the test. You are sleeping—sleeping—sleeping—"

"I'm not," Flynn protested, drowsily, just as his eyes closed and his head fell forward on his breast.

Stephen's soft hands stroked the detective's brow with a soothing movement; he never ceased repeating monotonously: "Sleep—sleep—I command you to sleep. Do you know who's talking to you, sergeant?"

"Dr. Burt." Flynn's voice was faint and disinterested.

"Why did you call to see me?"

"To get you to identify the photograph."

"Why was that necessary?"

Flynn hesitated, struggled a little, but lay back quietly again as Stephen's facile hands resumed their light massaging of his brow and cheeks, and he commanded: "Sleep, sergeant, sleep. You mustn't struggle.

You must not oppose me. Are you going to oppose me, sergeant?"

"No, doctor."

"Will you answer all my questions truthfully?"

"Yes, doctor." The tones were dead and lifeless, for Flynn slept a hypnotic sleep and only his subconscious mind was aware of his wakefulness.

"Why was it necessary that I should identify the photograph?"

"I've got to know before I act, doctor. The matron at San Quentin says it's Nance Belden but the photograph is on the passport of Penelope Gatlin. I've got to be sure before we arrange to deport her. If we deport the wrong person we're in for a suit; and the French police won't cooperate if the evidence ain't strong enough."

"Why do you want this girl?"

"She's made a fool out of me—and if I get her I'll shake her down. She's rich. She can afford to pay well to be let alone."

"You're not interested, then, in seeing her returned to prison."

"Not a damn bit, doctor. Why should I? That frail can't hurt anybody."

Stephen reached suddenly down and raised Flynn's right arm above his head. "Your right arm is paralyzed," he intoned. "You cannot move it. I defy you to move it. Try to move it."

Flynn's great body twisted, and a look of distress

came over his sleeping countenance. "Oh, Lord, I'm paralyzed!" he moaned. "I can't move it."

"You can't do anything until I tell you to, understand. I'm your master. Do you realize that? You must do everything I tell you to do."

"Yes, doctor."

Stephen sat down, lighted his pipe, and regarded P. Flynn with scientific interest. When his pipe was half smoked he said: "You are no longer paralyzed, sergeant. You can take your arm down now."

The arm came slowly down. Flynn had accomplished the impossible. For fifteen minutes his arm had been held aloft, rigid, motionless as a statue's.

"That name, Penelope Gatlin, is bad luck for you, Flynn," Stephen warned. "You must remember that always and never repeat it to a human soul. If you do, it may mean your death. Certainly it will mean great harm to you and your family. The oldest child will be kidnaped, tortured, and killed."

"Oh, God, no!" Flynn cried out in agony.

"You must forget Penelope Gatlin and Nance Belden. You must forget you ever heard those two names, understand? It is necessary if you are to be spared dreadful sorrow. Will you forget those two names?"

"Yes, doctor."

"You have already forgotten them. You can never remember them. Make up your mind now that you will never remember them again or mention those two names again as long as you live. You promise?"

"Yes, doctor. Oh, doctor, don't let them kidnap and torture my boy. I couldn't stand it, doctor."

"It will never happen if you obey me, sergeant. Now, what is the name of the girl whose photograph you showed me this evening?"

A curious slight spasm of distaste flashed across Flynn's face. He shuddered a little. "I don't know," he replied wearily. "I can't remember."

"What is the name of the lost heiress?"

"I don't know. I never heard of her."

"What is the name of the girl who escaped from San Quentin?"

"I don't know. You'll have to ask the warden."

Stephen picked up the little mirror and held it in the original position, then reached forward with his other hand and struck Flynn a smart slap on the top of the head.

"Wake up," he commanded.

Flynn came awake instantly and looked extremely foolish.

"Well, you didn't stand the test," Stephen assured him. "You stuck it out manfully, but those distended capillaries in your eyes couldn't stand the strain. Just as I suspected. You were falling asleep under the test, so I awakened you."

"The hell, I was! I don't remember being asleep."

"Oh, you didn't sleep, really, but if I'd let you, you would have fallen into profound slumber. Finish your drink."

Flynn finished it gratefully and, as alert as ever, returned to the subject they had been discussing just
before he had so adroitly and unsuspectingly been
thrown into the hypnotic sleep.

"Am I pretty bad, doc?"

"You're this bad, that if you do not take treatment
you will be in a bad way. I'll give you a prescription.
Get it filled at the corner drug store and take the medicine faithfully for a week. Then come and see me again
—here, not at my office."

"Thank you, doc. You're mighty kind. By the way, I
called to ask you some questions about a case—and
damn it, I can't seem to remember what it was. Good
Lord, doc, am I going crazy? I don't remember why I
called on you."

"You asked me to identify this passport photograph"
—and Stephen held out the little photo to Flynn, who
thrust it away. "That's bad luck, doc. Never mind.
You don't have to identify her. It's a matter of no importance."

He picked up his hat, bade Stephen good night, and
was ushered out by the butler.

Stephen stood, back to the fire, and smiled at the
retreating bulky form. "That was a dirty trick I played
on you, Pat Flynn," he chuckled. "You with your
arteries of a boy! But I've sealed that agile memory
of yours and I've sealed Mrs. Merton's, and with both
of you gone dry on the subject of Penelope Gatlin I
imagine the chief of detectives will not think of the

matter again either. Poor Flynn! He thinks he took some sort of eye test and will never know he talked out of his turn. And Lanny said I'd never make a detective."

CHAPTER FOURTEEN

TEN days after the cablegram to Penelope Gatlin had been sent, McNamara telephoned Lanny to ask if the girl had answered. Upon being told she had not, he said that was a very bad sign and was so cast down that Lanny felt sorry for him. Therefore, like all women who feel sorry for a man, she decided to feed him and invited him out to her house for dinner that night. She said Stephen would be there.

"That's no inducement," McNamara rumbled. "But I'll come anyhow. Thanks." He hung up and pondered the case of Penelope Gatlin, alias Nance Belden. He knew, of course, that in any negotiations between his inferiors in the department and the police of another state or country, his name was always signed to cablegrams and letters, since he was the chief. Therefore, if the chief of detectives or Detective-Sergeant Flynn had communicated with the prefect of police in Paris, any answer would, of course, come addressed to him, for which reason he could afford to refrain from exhibiting the slightest interest in the case to the captain of detectives.

The failure of the Paris police, however, to cable that they had taken the girl into custody, and were awaiting further instructions, could not be taken as evidence that they had not so acted. But if it did indicate a failure to take her into custody, McNamara could assume that Stephen's cablegram had beaten Flynn's to Paris, that Penelope had escaped, and that the Paris police were watching her house, waiting to apprehend her upon her return. Still, if the girl had escaped out of France, why hadn't she obeyed orders and cabled her present address?

McNamara's thoughts kept shuttling back to Penelope Gatlin all of that busy day. Finally, about five o'clock, he could stand it no longer and telephoned up to the detectives' room for Flynn to report to him.

"What job are you working on, Pat?" he demanded.

"This, that and the other thing, chief. Nothing big."

"How about that case I sent up to the chief of detectives recently. A Mrs. Rudolph Merton who called regarding her daughter who had disappeared two years ago." McNamara hadn't sent the case up at all, but he knew Flynn did not know this, so he elected to claim a real interest in it.

Flynn scratched his head. "Oh, yes. I did some work on that but didn't get anywhere. I called on the Merton woman and tried to get her to identify the girl's photograph, but she wouldn't or couldn't. She seemed scared to mention the girl's name, and finally she had hysterics. I think she's a nut. She said she didn't have any daughter that got lost."

"Probably a neurotic suffering from hallucinations. Did you get a line on the girl?"

"Sure. Traced her to an address in Paris."

"Under what name is she registered with the Paris police?"

McNamara was striving desperately to simulate an alert professional interest in the case in order to break down or destroy Flynn's suspicions, provided he had any.

Flynn scratched his red head and looked foolish. "Chief, I can't just recall it," he admitted, with some show of embarrassment. "I just can't."

"It was Penelope Gatlin, wasn't it?"

Flynn flinched a little, as from a blow, and a look of anxiety came into his eyes. "I don't know, chief. I can't remember the name."

"You're as bad as Mrs. Merton. What the devil's the matter with you?"

"I don't know, chief, except that I'm not interested in this case, I guess. Hand it over to some other dick. I'm not well lately."

"Nonsense. You're in the pink."

"Well, I don't think there's anything to the Merton case. The girl probably had to leave her nut of a mother or go cuckoo herself. I think we might as well drop it. Mrs. Merton won't cooperate, and we can't prove her daughter's lost if she says she never had a daughter."

"Very well, then, forget it, Pat. I was mildly curious, that's all." He dismissed Flynn. "By Jupiter, that fellow's getting too deep for me," he soliloquized. "The innocent face of the big bum! Him trying to put that line over on me! And acting like a scared kid! Is he cuckoo? Am I going cuckoo, too?"

He telephoned up to the captain of detectives. "What about that case of the lost heiress, reported by a Mrs. Rudolph Merton?" he demanded. "Has Flynn gotten anywhere with it?"

"We've dropped it, on Flynn's suggestion. He thinks that lost daughter isn't lost at all." He went on to explain in detail. McNamara grunted his comprehension and hung up. "Now, what is Flynn up to?" he pondered. "He's got the captain of detectives called off. Is he going to play a lone hand and shake the girl down when he finds her? If that's his little game I'll block it"—and he sent a cable to the prefect of police of Paris, thanking him for his kind services and informing him that he was no longer interested in Penelope Gatlin of 27, rue St.-Honoré and that surveillance of her might cease. Hoping for an early opportunity to reciprocate the courtesy, he signed himself by his official title, and on his way out to Lanny's house that night filed the cablegram personally and paid for it, reflecting the while that the first thing he knew he'd be out a month's salary on Penelope Gatlin.

Lanny, wearing a smart kitchen apron, ceased cooking dinner long enough to let him in. Stephen had not yet arrived, so McNamara went out into the kitchen with Lanny and sat down to watch her work, the while he related to her the latest news regarding the common nuisance. "And I hope," he added with a mild show of heat, "I've heard the last of that one. My soft heart," he explained, laying his hand on his umbilicus, "is always getting me into mischief. I still have that ex-convict holed up at my house, but he's no use to me now, so I'll have to get rid of him. He's an ex-soldier, so I'm arranging to get him into the Veterans' Hospital before my mother comes home."

Lanny gazed upon him very benignly. "You're a good man, Dan McNamara. How come you've never married?"

"If I had my mother would have lived with us," he declared a little sadly. "Mother's always been boss in her own house. She bossed my father before me, and if I didn't let her boss me she wouldn't be happy. So I've never married. No woman, Lanny, will stand for bossing unless she does it herself. How come you've never been married?"

Lanny sighed. "Nobody ever asked me."

McNamara sighed gustily; his eyes swept the kitchen linoleum. "My poor mother's very old and in bad health," he said.

"A man like you should have sons—fine, big, strapping manly sons—to enrich the world."

"How old are you, Lanny?"

"Well, I'm over forty-five."

"I'm forty-six myself." He sighed again. "I'm afraid poor mother won't live long." His eyes bored into Lanny. "You're a fine woman, Lanny—devil a finer. We might manage it."

"Manage what?"

"To put up with mother for the little time she has to live, God bless her. She was forty-three when she bore me. I'm the youngest in a family of seven, which is why she'll live with none of the others. I'm always the baby to her; always in need of her, the poor dear—so she thinks."

"I never could stand a left-handed proposal, Dan."

"Then here's my right hand on it, Lanny"—and he laid his great right paw in hers. "If it's sons you'd have, you old darlin', 'tis little time we have to waste."

A faint flush came to Lanny's slightly faded cheeks and a soft glow in her fine eyes. For the moment she was almost pretty. "What would Stevie do without me?" she murmured.

"He might go to hell—not wishing him any bad luck," McNamara retorted with spirit.

"Dan! How dare you?"

"It's been my observation, Lanny, that a woman without something to occupy her mind is in a poor way, even if she has a small house and a husband to look after. Husbands—that is, husbands like me—require little looking after. Breakfast and dinner and the bed made and his laundry sent out and a pressed suit in the closet—neither more nor less. You could continue to look after the doctor's office."

"That's a good formula, Dan, but it lacks one important ingredient."

"Name the lack and I'll get it."

"You're not in love with me."

"To hell I'm not!"

"You haven't said so."

"You're like all the women—forever putting dogs in windows, as my grandmother used to say—whatever she meant by that. I was in love once when I was a patrolman. She died—the Lord have mercy on her—and I've never looked at a woman since with love in my heart until I met you. Whether or not 'tis the real McCoy, I don't know, my dear, but I'll bet you a cooky 'tis a good substitute. At any rate," he added, with an odd wistfulness for such a big, homely man, "I'm not used to blandhering or passing words lightly on such a subject. Give me a yes or no answer."

"You great, lovable idiot," Lanny almost yelled. Advancing swiftly upon the chief she took his Cro-Magnon head in her arms and kissed his pompadour. "I'll risk your mother, Dan," she said softly. "All my life I've been looking for a man with a heart in his chest—and the day you first came to Stevie's office, with your big swaggering way and your blarney and your air of owning the world and everything in it I—I wondered if you were married. I'm no longer young, Dan. I have peculiar ways and I'm bossy, too—"

McNamara drew her face down and kissed it. "What a blessing I'm used to that, Lanny, and have learned to be kind to the aged. Here, quit pulling my hair, woman, or once the priest has mumbled over us I'll take a black-jack to you, you—you—quick-thinking, proud, independent criminal, you! If I did my duty I'd put the cuffs on you this minute!

"Huh-hum! I suppose you think I do spring dances in my shirt-tail night and morning as I face the same prospect, eh? Now, let me tell you something before you go too far. I do not like eggs, and if you can't make a good cup of coffee—well, it's not too late to back out."

Lanny's laughter had an hysterical note in it. This man was going to be so easy to get along with. A josher; a spoofer. All his days he'd be poking fun at her, making her forget she was no longer young, no longer good-looking. But he'd cherish her. She knew his type. A one-woman man—a type distinctly Celtic, faithful by first intention. He wasn't an Adonis, but he had a big, healthy, trim body and had not permitted himself to go to paunch. And he was highly intelligent. What a doctor he would have made! Patient with the helpless, ruthless with the malingerers, sympathetic with the hopeless. What oodles of mental therapy he could supply . . . the fierce, kindly, beaming eye of him and his big blue-black jowls. A great scar on his chin and four long white ones on his black poll . . . a fighting man but oh, how lovingly he could dandle babies on his knee . . . the sweet thing!

She stood, staring at him, thinking all these things, and she knew she was going to weep unless she said something. She had missed romance, but she had found love, and the knowledge was choking her. So she said:

"How about a little old-fashioned Bourbon cocktail, darling? All by ourselves, before Stevie comes."

"I could do with a bit of good spiritus frumenti, Lanny love. We'll drink to a long life and a happy one."

While she was mixing the cocktails Stephen rang the door-bell, but Lanny made him wait until she had mixed three.

"Will that fella be forever interfering in our lives, I wonder?" McNamara demanded with mock grouchiness.

"What's wrong with you, Lanny?" Stephen demanded querulously, when Lanny admitted him. "I rang half a dozen times." He felt that he must be querulous frequently in order to make Lanny happy.

"Do you good to wait once in a while," she snapped back at him. "Who do you think you are? The Akoond of Swat."

He followed her back into the kitchen. "Mac," he declared, "you have a proprietary air about you?"

"And well I may," Mr. McNamara replied pertly. "I've just popped the question to Lanny, and we've agreed to jump over the broomstick together. Oh, wirra, wirra, wirra, I'm an engaged man, and what do you think of that, doctor? Not that what you think matters a hoot in a hollow, but just to make conversation. If you don't like it you can lump it."

"I've been expecting this, Dan. She hasn't been worth a canceled postage stamp to me since she met you. Take her with my compliments. You save me the trouble of firing her. Of course I'll never get another Lanny, but—God's will be done."

"But I'm not going to leave you, Stevie darling. Oh, I couldn't leave my boy."

"Sometimes I think you're fond of me, Lanny."

Stephen held out his arms, and good old faithful Lanny ran straight into them, and they kissed each other, and the strangest thing—and most embarrassing to McNamara—happened. They had a nice, moist, happy little cry together. And then Stephen hugged McNamara and warned him solemnly that if he wasn't good to Lanny he, Stephen, would hypnotize him, just as he had hypnotized P. Flynn, and sell him the idea he was a poodle, so Lanny could kick him around at will.

"You what?" McNamara yelled. "You put the comother on Flynn?"

"Certainly. Flynn called on me to pump me in a kindly way and try to scare me into identifying Penelope's passport photo as that of Nance Belden. I got his mind off his business by scaring him into thinking he had arteriosclerosis; then I demanded a fake eye test, and with his mind in a subjective state with reference to anything I might tell him, I put him to sleep—although not into a deep sleep—by making him stare at a little mirror held six inches above the level gaze of his eyes. That strain would put an elephant to sleep. Since he didn't know he was being hypnotized, he didn't oppose me. Dan, he made a beautiful subject— as passive as a baby, and I secured quick control. He

told me all he knew—and that he intended to shake
Penelope down for keeping her out of San Quentin—"

"The red rat!"

"Don't worry about him. I commanded him to forget
he had ever heard of Nance Belden and Penelope Gatlin; I warned him that if he didn't forget them absolutely his eldest child would be kidnaped and tortured.
Of course, when I waked him he had perfect amnesia
for all that had taken place during the hypnotic state,
but the ideas I implanted in his subconscious mind are
there to stay, even if he doesn't know it. To forget
Penelope Gatlin and Nance Belden is now, with Flynn,
an acquired instinct. He will not remember because his
subconscious mind will forbid any conscious thought
on the subject. He will feel uneasy and apprehensive if
anybody else mentions those two names, but he will
not know why this is so. Why, I have Flynn's mind
hermetically sealed, just as I sealed Mrs. Merton's!
She has forgotten she ever had an adopted daughter,
and when Flynn interviewed her she had hysterics. As
for Penelope, two years ago she autohypnotized herself
into forgetting her adopted mother—into forgetting
she ever had one. And if the poor child should ever
come under my care I'll not take the trouble to wake
her up and cause her to remember."

"Three hundred years ago, in Salem, Massachu-
setts," said Dan McNamara, "you'd have been burned
for a witch—a devil with the evil eye. What are you
going to do about poor Pat Flynn's blood-pressure?"

"I prescribed some soda-mint tablets for him. They are quite without medicinal value, save possibly to an anguished stomach after a night out. He is to report back in a week, and when he does, something tells me his blood-pressure will have dropped twenty points. A week later it will be normal, and for the remainder of his life Flynn will be sending me all of his friends with high blood-pressure, and I'll have the devil's own job to get rid of them!"

"You're a sly, scheming, villainous vagabond, so you are!" McNamara declared.

"You keep quiet," Lanny commanded. "He's a darling and always was."

The door-bell rang insistently. "Now who can that be?" Lanny exploded peevishly.

"In the midst of life's sweetest moments," said McNamara, "we can always depend on somebody butting in like a disease. Don't stir, Lanny darling. You've been on your feet all day. Keep your eye on the dinner, and I'll open the door. If it's somebody wanting to sell you anything I'll ask him has he got a license and if he hasn't—"

He rolled out of the kitchen and down the hall. Then Stephen and Lanny heard the door slammed violently; there was a scuffle in the hall, and something—Lanny knew it to be the terra-cotta umbrella stand—crashed to the floor. Came McNamara's bull-fiddle voice: "Ah, ha! You would, would you? Well, just for that I'll cuff you."

He came into the kitchen a moment later leading by her handcuffed wrist none other than Penelope Gatlin. "She wouldn't kiss me first," he announced, "so I put the cuffs on her—the little vixen."

"Oh, Lanny, you *darling*. And Stevie, you *sweet-heart*," Penelope cried, and extended her manacled arms. Lanny dodged in under them and folded the girl to her heart. "You next, Stevie," Penelope ordered, and obediently Stephen lowered his head and the looped arms came around his neck and drew his face down, that Penelope might kiss him mightily. "And now, Dan," the girl cooed, and turned her face upward for the hearty smack he deposited on her ripe red lips. "Lanny first always, Dan."

"Was he jealous?" Lanny demanded.

"No, just romantic, Lanny dear. He couldn't help it. . . . Turn me loose, old funny-business, or I'll tell the world what a crooked chief of police you can be without half trying."

McNamara laughingly uncuffed her, and the quartet stood a moment staring at each other. It was one of those moments when words are quite superfluous. Then Penelope lifted the lid on a savory smelling skillet and coyly inspected its contents.

"Oh, dear," she sighed, "I'm so hungry! I came across in four days on the Bremen and was seasick all the way. Then I came west on the T.A.T. and had a sandwich and a cup of coffee for luncheon today. Got into Los Angeles and transferred immediately to a waiting ship on the Los Angeles-San Francisco air line —and that line doesn't serve any food. Got to the airport and was too excited to eat. I'm starved." She made a leap for Lanny and kissed her again, and then, because this remarkable young woman played no favorites, she hugged Stephen and McNamara once more and declared feelingly that it was simply wonderful to be home again.

" 'Simply wonderful to be home again,' says she," . McNamara muttered. "Come here to me, mavourneen, and tell Dan what your name is?"

"Nance Belden, of course."

"I thought so. Take the witness, doctor."

"Why didn't you cable us?" Stephen demanded, a trifle severely. Penelope's habit of appearing and disappearing without notice was uncanny, occult. It disturbed the established order of things, and Stephen was a very orderly man.

"I adore surprises, that's why. When I got Dan's cablegram it was midnight. The servants were in bed, so I packed two big suitcases, left expense money and salaries for three months on the table in the salon and motored to Berlin. Flew down to Bremen and caught the steamer an hour before she sailed. It's just about a week since then. Boys and girls, I've been on the jump."

"Why did you come back?" McNamara demanded.

"The proper place to hide oneself is in the spot one is supposed to have fled from in terror. I knew a man

once who spent hours searching for his spectacles, and
all the time they were on his silly nose."

"Woman," McNamara mourned, addressing Lanny,
"we're all weak. Let's have whatever you've got cooked,
so we can gather strength to think of what we'll do
with this one."

"What an adorable little tailored suit you have,
Penny," was all the attention Lanny paid to the chief's
appeal. "Did you buy it in Paris?"

"Yes, Lanny. Oh, I've got some presents for you all.
They're in my suitcase and it's in the hall."

"Dan," said Lanny and pointed a thumb toward the
hall. Obediently McNamara retrieved the suitcase, and
Penelope knelt on the kitchen floor and opened it. "A
solid silver teapot for you, Lanny. Very antique German, with a crest. Some poor baron must have had to
part with it after the war. And here's a big blue porce-
lain pipe for Stephen and a gold-rimmed, real amber
cigar-holder for Dan. Do you like this string of cut
crystal beads? They're really quite swagger."

She hung them against Lanny's throat.

"Who are they for?" McNamara queried.

"For the matron at San Quentin. She's such a dear."

"The Lord ha' mercy on us," McNamara almost
moaned. " 'For the matron at San Quentin,' says she.
'She's such a dear,' says she. Don't tell me, Nance, you
haven't brought something for Sapphire Susie. Why,
she would be broken-hearted if she thought you'd overlooked her, after all she's done for you."

"She's been paid off long ago," the girl replied with some asperity. "She was well paid, too. Dan, what have you done with my motorboat?"

"I had it stored in a boat yard and fixed up as good as new. What else could I do with it? The boat was never registered in the custom house, and if I'd gone joy-riding in it without the official numbers on the bow the coast guard would have picked me up."

"The person in whose name that boat might have been registered would have been out of luck," Penelope sighed a little wearily. "I'll have to sell my boat now. I'm very short of funds, and can't get any until the next semiannual collection of my income. Lanny, don't let them stand around staring at me and asking me questions. I'm hungry and *so* tired. Can I have my same little bed tonight?"

"You can have anything and everything you want, my poor dear."

"I want Stephen," came the answer, faintly tired, and the girl went to him and leaned her sleek black head against his breast, while her arms went around his neck. "I've missed you so, Stephen. I'd like to get shot again, so you could come and dress the wound and talk so nice and kind to me, the way you used to do. I'm lonely."

Stephen held her close with his left arm, and his right hand came up and cautiously fingered her poor nose. "God's on our side, Lanny," he told his nurse. "Tomorrow I want you to arrange for a room in St.

Dunstan's Hospital. We'll get Boyd to operate. None better. Poor child! She's not herself tonight. She's been through too much excitement lately. That cablegram shocked her. But with a night's rest and the feeling of security that will be hers now she knows she's with friends, she'll be herself tomorrow." He tweaked the sad nose. "And we've all been so amazed at your sudden reappearance we haven't thanked you for the presents. You're a dear, kind, thoughtful girl. I love my pipe. It's going to be the ideal pipe for my study at home."

"I'll start using my cigar-holder right after dinner," McNamara added. "You were a sweet one to think of old Mac and you so far away and the wide ocean between us and all."

"And the old silver teapot is priceless," Lanny said.

"I'm glad you liked them. I love you all and I want you all to love me. Please, Stephen, do I have to go away any more?"

"No, not any more, my dear."

"And you'll fix my nose? I wanted to have it done in Paris, but when Mac sent me that cablegram I couldn't of course. I have sketches of the exact nose I want. Can I have just the nose I want, Stephen?"

"Yes, little wanderer. And when that's done you shall have just the kind of home you want, and think the kind of thoughts that will make you happy. You've been lost in the woods, poor babe, but I'll lead you out into the loveliest sunshiny meadow imaginable."

McNamara had, throughout this scene, felt a lump in his throat. He glanced at Lanny and saw the tears of sympathy in her brave, kindly eyes; so to avert a scene he growled huskily:

"When do we eat?"

CHAPTER FIFTEEN

FOR the first time since Penelope Gatlin, alias Nance Belden, had come under his notice, Stephen Burt had a reasonable opportunity to examine the girl, when, following dinner, Penelope, Lanny, Dan McNamara, and Stephen retired to the drawing-room. Despite the strain of her record-breaking journey from Europe, Penelope was not so tired that she wished to retire early. She joined in the general conversation, and Stephen noticed that she seemed inclined to be argumentative, but her arguments indicated no cogent thought; frequently she employed the patois of the underworld; her language was racy and idiomatic. He noticed that her laugh was sudden, loud—the laugh of a vulgarian. She was nervous; her hands twined and intertwined continuously, she moved about the room a great deal, and finally came to rest on Stephen's knees. She looked into his eyes searchingly for a long time and then said accusingly: "You don't care for me."

"Why do you think that, Nance?"

"Because nobody could love a girl with a nose like mine."

"Did you bring back the sketches that Parisian artist made of you?"

She bounced off his lap and hurried upstairs, to

return presently with a portfolio filled with sketches. There was one crayon drawing of her as she was. A half-dozen additional sketches were copies of the first, with the exception of the nose. The artist had fitted into her features a nose of his own design, and viewed in profile, some of his creations lent to the girl's face an aspect of singular beauty and sweetness.

"I like this one best," Stephen decided. "The patrician nose does you justice. Going to come over tomorrow and give you the most searching physical examination you've ever had," he decided. He drew her over to him and kissed her on the cheek, paternally. "You're a nice, sweet, lovable girl, Penelope," he assured her as if she were a little girl, "and the shape of your nose isn't taken into consideration by the sort of people whose love and approval you desire. And you can get along very well without the love and approval of any other sort. Dan and Lanny and I all love you and we want you to love us. We're your only real friends, and you wouldn't do anything to hurt us, would you?"

"I'd rather die, Stephen."

"Fine. You're tired now, so suppose you run upstairs to bed, and tomorrow, when you wake up, you'll be refreshed and happy and we'll be able to discuss the making over of this poor nose. Kiss us all good night."

Penelope dutifully obeyed, and as she was starting up the stairs Stephen said: "And don't forget to say your prayers."

She grimaced disdainfully. "You must think I'm a nut—saying my prayers. I've been prayed to death."

"By whom?"

"I don't know, but by somebody. It makes me ill."

"That was the subconscious revulsion to her adopted mother coming out," Stephen told McNamara. "Mrs. Merton had a strong religious mania. That girl's a mighty healthy specimen," he continued. "I noticed, when I was dressing the wound in her shoulder, that her skin is soft and silky, not rough and dry as in the case of psychopathic personalities. Everything about her seems to indicate sound ancestry, and I'm more than ever convinced that her mental disturbance is not organic. However, that's a lead we can run down after we've fixed her nose."

"We'll not fix it in this city, my boy." Thus McNamara.

"Why not?"

"Because when that girl is well she'll probably elect to live her life here, and I don't want a soul in this city, with the exception of ourselves, to know that once she had a saddle nose and a dual personality."

"We can trust the ethical integrity of the man I purpose—"

"I'll trust nobody but myself—and then not too much. Where is the best plastic surgeon in this country?"

"In New York City."

"Lanny, I'll ask the police commissioner for a sixty-day leave of absence. We'll be married at once and take this child to New York with us, put her in a hospital there and have the job done. While it's being done we'll have our honeymoon."

"Three is a crowd—on a honeymoon," Stephen warned.

"It's nothing of the sort," Lanny defended. "Stevie, you mind your own business. Dan and I know our way about."

"Indeed? Well, just because you're so contumacious, I'm going to tell you something. If I hadn't promoted this engagement, you and Dan would not now be engaged. Dan had you up on a pedestal—which is where you never belonged—and you're so naturally man-shy you never even learned the rudiments of the come-on as practiced by the dullest, so I talked the matter up."

"You didn't talk it up to me."

"No, but I listened sympathetically when you raved about what a grand man Dan McNamara was, and my neck is still stiff from nodding agreement. I told Dan you were crazy about him and worked up his courage—"

"You're a liar," McNamara charged, feebly and without malice.

"Dan McNamara is one man who doesn't have to have help with his courage or thinking," Lanny declared pridefully. "And you do, Stephen Burt. You're adept at lording it over your befuddled patients, but Rebecca P. Lanning is a horse of another color."

"I think I'll go home," Stephen retorted, and went.

He was back in the morning with the impedimenta of his profession. Penelope greeted him gravely. "Good morning, Dr. Burt."

He started. The strident note of Nance Belden was gone from her voice. She spoke now in the low, level tone of the girl of breeding. Then she sat down, and they conversed for half an hour on topics of general interest, but during that time she did not move once from her seat. Her vocabulary was free of underworld expressions, her diction perfect, her sentences grammatical.

"You have had a good night's rest, Miss Gatlin," he ventured.

She nodded, smiling a little. "I am not at all nervous this morning, Dr. Burt. When I am very tired, or excited about something, I am always horribly nervous."

"And you get dreadfully depressed, do you not?"

She nodded. "So depressed that at times I want to die."

"Well, we might as well start your physical examination. I'm going to try to ascertain why you can't be cheerful always. There's a reason, of course, for your nervousness and depression, so I want to examine you very meticulously and see if your trouble can be charged up to some physical condition. Let me feel your pulse."

It was eighty-three, full and strong.

Stephen's examination of the girl was as complete as modern medical science could make it, and when the last laboratory report came in three days later he called Lanny in to discuss the girl.

"With the exception a subnormal chest expansion, Lanny, that girl is without doubt the healthiest young woman I have ever examined. Her sole physical defect is her nose. But for that I think she'd be a husky little athlete right now. She told me she always wanted to excel in tennis, golf, and dancing—well, of course she'd want to excel in something. She couldn't compete in good looks. I'll write up my report on her, and you can hand a copy of it to the man who is to do the operation. I've wired him that I was sending on a patient, and he has agreed to care for her. Has Mac been given a leave of absence?"

Lanny nodded.

"When are you and he to be married?"

"Tomorrow. We're flying to Reno to avoid the three-day notice of intention to marry demanded by the California law."

"Penelope flying with you?"

"Naturally. She's my bridesmaid!"

"Who's going to give the bride away?"

"Nobody. Dan and I are too old to stand for a long-drawn-out marriage ceremony."

"Well, I suppose I'm stuck for a wedding present. How much money have I got in the bank?"

"Approximately twenty thousand. I'm going to buy you some Argentine bonds today. There's no reason why those bonds should be selling at eighty-nine—"

"Lanny, you're mercenary. I don't care for a disser-
tation on bonds. Draw yourself a check for ten thousand and spend it all in riotous living. Give old Dan a
real blow-out—"

"Stevie, you're mad!"

"Quiet, please. Love from the boss, Lanny, and no
back talk from you. And for heaven's sake do get me
a half-way intelligent nurse to take your place while
you're away."

"I've engaged Miss Ordway."

"Horrible. Her face would stop a parade. She's
efficient, but terrible to look at."

The tears were welling in Lanny's eyes. "Oh, Stevie,
I want you to be safe—while I'm away," she choked.
"No hoity-toity—young thing—with her sweet smile—
and winning ways—and you such a—softy—oh, Stevie,
Stevie, I can't bear to leave you. If I do, something
dreadful will happen to you." And Lanny laid her head
on her desk and sobbed quite heartily.

However, Stephen knew what was good for Lanny.
"You make me ill," he said coldly. "You carry on like
a girl of sixteen."

Instantly Lanny was furious. "You don't appreciate
me," she charged.

"Be still. Where's the check-book? On an occasion
such as the present I suppose I should sign the check
myself."

"It wouldn't do any good if you did, darling. You've
never registered your signature at your bank and you

have no authority to sign checks on your own bank account. How funny!" and Lanny commenced to laugh. "How lucky I thought of that before leaving!"

Thereupon Stephen put both arms around her and kissed her three times and told her she was as the shadow of a rock in a weary land; that she was very dear to him; that whatever she did was O.K. with him and he'd miss having his daily fight with her; and finally so softened her that she consented to let him fly to Reno and give the bride away. It developed that she had always wanted him to do this but loathed putting him to so much trouble.

At the expiration of his leave, McNamara returned to duty, but Lanny remained with Penelope in New York. Performed by a master, the operation had proved successful thus far. The actual work of the operation had been the least of it; the subsequent care of the bone and skin graft, and the surgeon's artistry in reshaping the nose were what required time and patience. Lanny reported that the patient would not be discharged for at least three months more.

"How did Penelope approach the operation?" Stephen queried of McNamara.

"Happily. Not a whit nervous. Lanny had complete control over her." He grinned. "I passed as her Uncle Dan and the wife as Aunt Lanny. Lanny saw to it that the girl didn't do any talking while the doctor was present."

"You're a good fellow, Dan."

"Well," McNamara admitted humorously, "it wasn't much of a honeymoon, I'll admit. However, we'd set our hands to the job and we couldn't turn back, God help us."

"Well, you have this consolation, my friend. Your job is over, and mine will commence when Lanny returns with the girl."

"D'ye think you can pull her through, lad?"

"I'm sure I can, Dan. A psychoneurosis generally is impossible to cure unless you know its causative factors and can remove them. If you can do that, it's as simple as removing a wart. Dan, have you looked up the girl's ancestry?"

"I have not."

"Then do so immediately. We might run into a situation that will shed a bright, effulgent beam of light on my job."

"The attorney that handled Gatlin's affairs ought to be a good man to start with, Stephen. I'll motor to San José tomorrow and look him up. The bank will know who he is."

The bank president did know the name of the attorney, but added the disconcerting information that the man had been dead six years. McNamara thereupon called the attorney's widow to ask if she still retained her late husband's files. He had a faint hope that if she would permit him to look into the Gatlin file he might find a clue. He was informed, to his amazement, that about two years and a half before, Mrs. Merton had called upon her, asked for the file and had been given it.

There was but one club in the city—the Elks—and McNamara wondered if Theodore Gatlin had belonged to that. He discovered Gatlin had, and from the dining-room steward, who remembered Theodore Gatlin very well, he ascertained the names and addresses of three men with whom Gatlin had seemed very friendly.

Of these three men, one was dead and the others were unable to shed any light upon the parentage of Gatlin's adopted daughter, although one man had a hazy recollection that the child's father had been an army officer and had been killed in the Philippines. The chief's questionings, however, elicited the names of two women who had been friendly with Mrs. Gatlin, so Mc-Namara called upon both. They could furnish him no information beyond the fact that Mrs. Gatlin despised the child Penelope; that she had never been enthusiastic about the adoption; that she had never been kind to the girl; that Gatlin and Penelope had been inseparable pals. They had a feeling that Mrs. Gatlin, while apparently delighting in persecuting her husband, was, nevertheless, insanely jealous of his love for his adopted daughter; that, up to the day of her accident, Penelope had been a bright, healthy, normal child, fun-loving and affectionate and humorous. She had attended a private school and they gave McNamara the name of it. He did not bother to call upon the school authorities, however. He was satisfied they could tell him nothing and he was not interested in a perusal of Penelope's scholastic record. He knew it would be excellent.

He reported to Stephen somewhat depressed, because he had returned, as he thought, without a scintilla of worth-while information. Stephen, however, thought otherwise. Nor was he the least bit discouraged. "I'll have to question Mrs. Merton again," he decided. He rang for Miss Ordway. "Telephone to Mrs. Merton," he ordered, "and tell her I wish she'd drop in here some day soon. Tell her that for the sake of my own self-satisfaction I'd like the latest report on her health."

"What are you going to do?" McNamara asked.

"Hypnotize her again, of course. I've got to release her from the mental inhibition I set upon her in the case of her adopted daughter. Otherwise she'll not talk."

A minute later Miss Ordway entered the room. "Mrs. Merton says she will be down in half an hour, doctor."

Stephen smiled. "When she arrives, Dan, you step out into the nurse's office until I have her under control; then I'll admit you. I think you'll be vastly interested in listening to the tale I will unfold. Besides, I want you to take copious notes."

True to her promise, Mrs. Merton fluttered into Stephen's consultation room forty minutes later. "Oh, Dr. Burt," she whined, "I'm so glad you've sent for me. Really, you're the only doctor that can do anything for me—the only one I can trust. My insomnia is worse than ever," she wailed. "Oh, doctor, do you think I'm going crazy?"

"Not at all, not at all," he soothed her. "You are excited over nothing. But you are in a highly nervous condition, of course, and until you have settled down it would be useless for me to attempt to examine you. If you could have a little nap for, say, half an hour on the couch in the next room I'm sure you would awaken much refreshed."

"Oh, if I could only sleep half an hour, doctor, if I only could! But it's quite impossible."

"Nonsense, my dear lady. We doctors have ways of inducing sleep even in the most obstinate insomnia."

At his command she lay down on the couch, and Stephen placed a cushion under her head. Employing the appropriate method of inducing the hypnotic sleep, he had her drowsy within three minutes; at the end of seven minutes he had induced light hypnotism; in ten minutes she had passed into the more profound state, and Stephen summoned McNamara, gave him a pad and pencil and silently indicated a chair.

Mrs. Merton, however, was aware of his presence. "Who's there?" she demanded drowsily.

"Dr. McNamara, Mrs. Merton. I have called him in to confer with me on your case."

"You are so kind, Dr. Burt."

He resumed his passive stroking of her forehead and cheeks; in a low, monotonous tone he commanded her to answer all his questions. Then suddenly:

"Have you thought of your daughter, Penelope, of late?"

A grimace of distress flitted across the beautiful face. "No, you told me not to."

"I release you from that promise. You are to think about her now. No distress or bad luck will attend the thinking while you are with me, understand? I command you to think about her—to remember her and to answer truthfully all of my questions regarding her."

"Yes, doctor."

"Why did you and Mr. Gatlin adopt her?"

"He wanted a baby and I couldn't give him one."

"Could you, if you had cared to?"

"Yes, doctor."

"How old was Penelope when you adopted her?"

"About a month."

"Where did you find her?"

"In the Infants' Shelter in San Francisco."

"Did you know who her parents were before you decided to adopt her?"

"Yes, doctor. A Captain and Mrs. Ronald Elliot."

"Why did the Elliots abandon their baby?"

"The captain was killed by the Moros and his wife died in childbirth. They had no relatives, or if they had, the relatives couldn't afford to take the baby or they didn't care to. So we took it."

"Do you remember what branch of the service the captain was in?"

"He was a captain of cavalry."

"When you and Mr. Gatlin adopted Penelope, did you have any written record of her parentage?"

"We had a letter from the matron at the Infants' Shelter—the one she first wrote about the baby. And we had a letter from the doctor who attended Mrs. Elliot at St. Dunstan's hospital, and some letters from old neighbors of the Elliots?"

"Why did you get the letters from the old neighbors?"

"Theodore was concerned about the baby's ancestry. He wanted to make certain it was the best."

"And was it the best?"

"I do not know. It satisfied him. I wasn't much interested."

"What has become of all the records pertaining to Penelope?"

"I burned them."

"Why?"

"To keep Penelope from getting them."

"Then she wanted them, did she not?"

"Yes, doctor. She demanded them."

"When was this?"

"On her eighteenth birthday."

"How did it happen that she waited until her eighteenth birthday before demanding them?"

"Up until then she thought she was our own flesh and blood."

"Ah!" Stephen glanced meaningly at McNamara.

"Why did you burn these records rather than give them to Penelope?"

"I hate her."

"When you refused to give them to her, what happened?"

"She cried and laughed and screamed and attacked me. She said she hated me. She called me a monster. Finally she fainted, and I had the maid put her to bed and lock her in her room."

"Did you give Penelope any information at all regarding her parentage?"

There was a slight hesitation. "I lied to her. I wanted to hurt her because she wouldn't recognize my moral right to half of Theodore's estate. So I told her she had Negro blood in her veins."

"What made you invent such a tale?"

"Penelope is a decided brunette. I thought even if she did not believe me my statement would create in her mind a doubt and a fear that would drive her crazy."

"What happened after that, Mrs. Merton?"

"In the morning she was gone."

"How did she go?"

"She tied sheets and blankets together and made a rope."

"Have you seen her since?"

"No."

"Is she dead?"

"I do not know. I hope so."

Stephen turned to Dan. "Any questions, Dan?"

McNamara shook his head owlishly. He had never been present at this sort of third degree before. "I can revive most of the record—perhaps all of it," he answered finally. "The captain's record is in the army files; when he married, a notice of it appeared in the Army and Navy Journal, and between the information that old file will contain and what I can get out of the officers who soldiered with the captain I'll get a pretty complete picture."

Stephen resumed his cross-examination.

"Did you ever beat Penelope?"

"Yes, doctor."

"Did you ever pinch her and slap her and lock her up?"

"Yes, doctor."

"Wake the fiend up and send her home," McNamara roared.

"I will—as soon as I lock up my memory of Penelope," Stephen replied, and proceeded to do so. But he went further. He impressed upon the subject the fact that she was not ill at all; that she was organically sound; that she only imagined she could not sleep; he commanded her to be healthy and happy and accept whatever happened smilingly. He commanded her very earnestly to forget that she had ever heard of him, Stephen; she was never to return to his office. Then he awakened her, as McNamara departed, gave her a long look, felt her pulse, told her she was much improved and handed her some soda-mint tablets. She departed happy.

"Well," McNamara demanded, when he and Stephen found themselves alone again, "what do you think of that one for a hell-cat?"

"I do not think, my dear Dan. We merely accept such people as we accept sunlight and rainfall. The world is quite filled with them, and men like them, too. Drop them in the midst of idyllic peace and decency and gentleness and within twenty-four hours they make an uproar."

"Do you think you'll see any more of this woman, Stephen?"

"I hope not. I hope the hypnotic suggestion I gave her is strong enough to overcome her acquired instinct for illness."

"Were the things she told you illuminating, my boy?"

"Very. I suspected most of them, and she confirmed my suspicion. We know now that Penelope is of sound ancestry. Her father was not a neurotic. If he hadn't been a normal, gallant fellow and physically fit he would never have become a captain of cavalry. He was killed in action—and in all probability it wasn't his first action. But we have arrived at a starting point, Dan—the reason for the mental shock that gave Penelope a dissociated personality."

"I didn't get that—quite, Stephen."

"You should have. For some reason best known to

themselves the Gatlins foolishly kept from Penelope the fact that she was not their own flesh and blood.

"However, while we have definitely established the date of the mental shock and the character of the shock, we have also established the causative factors leading up to the shock. Penelope had a most unhappy childhood. From earliest childhood she was the victim of bitter, rebellious thoughts. Silently and fiercely she rebelled against her fate, but there was nothing she could do about it. Then that baseball wrecked her nose. This was a mental and physical shock. The separation and divorce of the Gatlins was another terrible shock, because she lost Gatlin and there was nobody to protect her, even a little bit, from her adopted mother. And Gatlin's death was a severe shock. Then, as she emerged from childhood into maidenhood, the knowledge that her nose made her hideous became an obsession.

"Now, Dan, by this time there was no further necessity for concealing the facts of the child's birth. Gatlin, dead, had left his entire estate in trust to Penelope, and on her eighteenth birthday she was free to do as she pleased. She could leave her hell-cat of an adopted mother now. She carried her own check-book. The knowledge that she was not flesh and blood of the beloved Gatlin came as a terrible shock, and with it, of course, came other terrifying speculations."

"More piling on of the inferiority complex," McNamara interrupted. "And she cracked under it. Went into hysterics and attacked the devil of a woman who was the author of all of her misery. Then she made up her mind to forget her—and she did."

"A clear case of autohypnosis, Dan. Now you've got to run down the record of our Penelope and that of her parents. She must have it and it must be proof of the most convincing character, because such proof is necessary to her mental tranquillity. If we remove the unhappiness and substitute happiness she'll get well."

"Well," said McNamara, "I'll be back presently with the girl's record, and then—"

"Out of the darkness into the sunlight, Mac."

"Well, the next one I find in the darkness will stay there," the chief growled. "I couldn't go through another experience like this one without having a dual personality myself."

CHAPTER SIXTEEN

THE absence of the capable Lanny was a constant reminder to Dr. Stephen Burt of his sole experiment to date in a case of dual personality. He yearned with an alert scientific yearning to get to work on Penelope Gatlin, and when Dan McNamara appeared at the office one day, he saw by the satisfied smirk on the McNamara countenance that all had gone well.

"Let me see the documents," Stephen demanded.

McNamara handed them over. "Sound stock on both sides, I should say."

"Well, you've done your full duty and have kept the police of various cities busy for a few days," said Stephen. "You are dismissed with thanks. What do you hear from Lanny?"

"She'll be home next week. The skin graft on the girl's nose was a complete success. No sign of the operation will be noticeable in a month."

"And how does the girl feel about it?"

"She's crazy about her new nose and spends hours examining it in a hand mirror."

Stephen smiled. "She would!"

"Lanny says the girl's been her real self more than half the time since that first look."

"She would be. The knowledge that she is no longer hideous is helping to displace the old unhappiness and depression. And now I'm going to add to her happiness by sending her on this record, which I shall supplement with a report of my own on her case, pieced together from hearsay, gossip and the admissions of Mrs. Merton. She'll read it and study it, and in this convincing proof that she is not what Mrs. Merton told her she was, she'll probably get well without any further attention from me. These cases are simple, Dan. All you have to do is to discover the cause and remove it. Nature does the rest. She had an unhappy childhood, but she can now look forward to a happy womanhood, with all the money she needs to supplement that happiness. She will have no more rebellious thoughts, because the despot, her adopted mother, is wholly lost to her and can do her no further harm. Her black moods of depression—and no doctor can fathom the depth and profundity of those moods —will not come again, because she is organically and mentally sound and the product of a sound ancestry, with decency and longevity on both sides of her family."

"But she knows she was an inmate of San Quentin, doctor, and will not this knowledge depress her? She'll remember she was a convicted thief."

"She will, of course, feel great shame when fully restored to her normal personality. In her other personality, with her acquired instincts of morality and

convention smothered in her subconscious mind, she
has, of course, no sense of remorse or shame. She is
as natural as an animal then—thoroughly unmoral on
certain points, swayed entirely by conscious impulse
and free from the mental conflict that arises in
the mind of a normal person when confronted with
the impulse to commit a crime—the conflict between the
subconscious or acquired instincts of morality and the
conscious impulse to be immoral. I think that when I
have explained this to her she will understand just what
her mental condition was, and find in that an excuse
sufficiently substantial to overcome her chagrin and
sorrow. And her fear that the world will discover her
sorry record will, I feel certain, be alleviated by her
knowledge that it would be impossible for anybody
who knew her as saddle-nosed Nance Belden to recognize her as good-looking Penelope Gatlin. She will
realize that nobody, save you, Lanny, and myself,
know that Nance Belden and Penelope Gatlin were
one and the same person.

"Well, all I've got to say, young fella m'lad," the
admiring McNamara declared, "is that you're one hell
of a smart man!"

Some two weeks later, Lanny walked in on Stephen,
who glanced up at her without enthusiasm. "Well,"
he declared acidly, "you've certainly taken your time
about getting back on the job."

Lanny beamed happily and captured him for a rib-
cracking hug and four fervent kisses.

"You're looking mighty particular, Lanny," he observed. "Happy?"

"Stevie, dear, I never knew there was such happiness in the world. Dan has found a capable woman to look after his old mother and has left her the mistress of his old home. He's moved over to my house—the lamb!"

"He's a big buck goat, but never mind that. Where's Penelope?"

"She's gone back to Paris—on a new passport."

"Well, well, well," Stephen chid her, "tell me things."

"Stevie, she's as lovely as a May morning, and she's just as good as she can be."

"And the operation?"

"A phenomenal success. That surgeon is a marvel. Her new nose is adorable, and I defy anybody to know that she has had an operation. Of course," Lanny added, with a return to her old masculine habit of expressing herself, "she could never stand a good sock on the nose."

"What's she going to do in Paris?"

"Close out her apartment and dismiss her servants."

"And then she's coming back to San Francisco?"

Lanny nodded. "How do you stand Miss Ordway, Stevie?"

"Rather well, I'm sorry to say. She's very competent and much more tactful than you. At least she hasn't tried bullying me yet."

For that remark Lanny kissed him again. "And do you want me back, darling?" she queried.

"There you go, fishing for a compliment. Of course I do, but—it isn't necessary, if you'll agree to look after my accounts and my money. You could come in once a week—"

"Not for a great many weeks, Stevie."

He glanced up at her sharply. "How come, Lanny?"

Lanny's face was the color of an old rose. "I'm going to have a baby," she whispered.

And then Stephen Burt stood up and took dear old Lanny in his strong young arms and hugged her. But he said nothing. For what was there to say? At last she was going to have her little slice of life! She wouldn't be lonely any more, despairing, filled with forebodings of the future.

"Of course," Lanny said presently, "you'll be the baby's godfather?"

He nodded. Of course. That was his privilege.

CHAPTER SEVENTEEN

THREE months passed—to Stephen Burt remarkable by reason of the fact that Mrs. Rudolph Merton did not call upon him. He wondered if the hypnotic suggestion he had given her was really efficacious, so at last, to satisfy his curiosity, he telephoned Rudolph Merton to ask him how his wife was.

"I don't know," Merton replied complacently. "She's gone."

"Dead?"

"No such luck, doctor. She's gone to Southern California to join a new religious sect. It has a colony out on the fringe of the San Bernardino desert and there's a wily prophet in command. I think he's collecting liberally from Mrs. Merton."

"And what are you doing about it, Mr. Merton?" Stephen asked.

"I'm subsidizing the prophet so he'll stay in business ten months longer. Mrs. Merton has deserted me, thank God, but she has to be away a year before I can secure a divorce on the grounds of desertion. That's the easiest way out, isn't it, doctor? The prophet comes high—a thousand a month—but I can afford to pay for my fancies."

"I gather you're not broken-hearted, Mr. Merton."

"Such sorrow as I feel now would be delirious delight compared with what I'd feel if she came back to me. My lawyer thinks I'll escape without the payment of alimony, as Mrs. Merton has private means ample to support her."

"I congratulate you, Mr. Merton. Good-by and good luck to you. You deserve it."

As Stephen hung up the telephone receiver, chuckling, Miss Ordway brought in his mail. In it he found a registered parcel that had been through the customs house, with duty prepaid on it. It contained the finest and most expensive combination stop-watch and time-piece he had ever seen, and a note that read:

Dear Dr. Burt:

I know it would not be *au fait* for me to ask you for a bill for professional services, for I realize that what you did for me was done as one human being to another and quite without thought of financial remuneration. Moreover, I prefer to remain forever your debtor. You will never know what you have done for me. Christ, restoring life to the dead son of the widow of Nain, performed no greater miracle than did you in restoring life and happiness to my dead soul. I would try to thank you if words were not so pitifully inadequate to express the profundity of my gratitude. Will you not please accept the enclosed trifle as a token of that gratitude and add one more debt to those already owed you by me?

It is not easy to learn to live with my secret, now

that I have found it out. I am trying to regard the past as one harks back in memory to a very serious illness. Some day, when I have achieved sufficient courage, I am coming back to San Francisco. I am curious about my other self—that dark self, evolved from darkness. There are blanks in my life. Perhaps you can fill them in. Perhaps you will not care to, knowing that they are better left blank. I do not think, however, that I was ever terribly wicked. If so, I have no recollection of it.

Your Grateful

PENELOPE.

"Old Mother Nature is speaking to Penelope," he soliloquized, and replaced his father's old watch with the one Penelope had sent him. "Give Nature a chance —give her an even break—and she'll prove herself the greatest physician of all."

After office hours that night he went down to the cable office and cabled Penelope:

Come home and let me iron out the few remaining wrinkles so your life will be as smooth as you could wish. The watch is wonderful. Thanks and I think you are very wonderful too. Love as usual.

STEPHEN.

It occurred to him to tuck that last phrase in for good measure. Love—not merely the love of a man for a woman but the love that is a fine friendship—was, he knew, very necessary to Penelope. She had been

denied it for so many years. She must, he knew, be
assured that in all the world, somebody really cared;
that, having cared once and demonstrated it, the lov-
ing solicitude would not be withdrawn. Nobody knew
better than he the wreckage that kindness and love denied can make of human lives; never a day passed
without leaving him evidence of this. Reflecting on
this as he drove home, a wave of loneliness swept over
him.

He was not getting quite his little slice of life.
Money, success, the joy of accomplishment, professional standing and the respect of his colleagues, he
had, plus some good friends and true. But were they
true? It occurred to him that he had never tested them.
There had never been any necessity to do this—ah,
yes, there was Lanny and good old McNamara. These
two he had seen tested . . . no doubt as to their quality.

He decided not to dine alone. It would be far better
to drop in unannounced on Lanny and Dan, take pot
luck for dinner, quarrel with Lanny, spoof with Dan,
and warm himself in the reflected glow of their love
and the new love that was coming to bless them soon
and remove the terror of old age—yes, he must look
well after Lanny.

"It'll be a boy," Stephen reflected, "and I'm sure
he'll be as ugly as Dan. But his soul will be sweet.
Yes, I'm sure of that."

CHAPTER EIGHTEEN

I T was late fall. Stephen had just returned from his
vacation; it was his first day back at the office, and
he was a bit rebellious at the flood of patients that
awaited him. He finally got rid of the last one at half
past five, and following his custom, settled back for a
pipeful of tobacco, when Miss Ordway entered.

"There's a young lady calling," she announced, "A
Miss Elliot."

"I don't know her, Miss Ordway. A prospective
patient?"

"I imagine she is. I didn't ask."

"Tell her it's beyond office hours and suggest that
she call tomorrow."

Miss Ordway departed to deliver the message, but
returned presently to say that the young lady begged
to be permitted to see him; that it would be inconveni-
ent for her to call next day. "Very well, show her in,"
he acquiesced irritably, "but remember Professor
Finnegan if she stays too long."

Miss Elliot entered. Stephen rose and waved her to
a chair, then sat down and appraised his new patient
for an appreciable moment. Then: "Well, Miss Elliot,
what seems to be the trouble?"

"Does my general appearance indicate to you, even remotely, that I am one who requires the services of a neurologist and psychiatrist?"

Her voice was low, cultured, with a resonant melody in it.

Stephen smiled. "Scarcely. What is it, then? A subscription to something?"

"How astute you are, doctor. I am soliciting subscriptions to a fund designed to furnish expert medical attention to a very deserving public servant. In fact, I believe you know him—he was once a patient of yours. I refer to Detective-Sergeant Patrick Joseph Flynn."

"I know him, Miss Elliot. What's wrong with Flynn?"

"His blood-pressure is extraordinarily high and unless—"

"Nothing doing, Miss Elliot," Stephen interrupted. "I admit I sold this terrible Flynn the notion that he had high blood-pressure, but I did that for a reason I do not care to explain. The man has the arteries of a boy. What's Flynn to you? You do not live in his world."

"I lived in it for a few months once."

"And who," said Stephen, "might you be?"

"You have my name. What I want to know is this: Are you ashamed to take me out to dinner?"

"No, of course not." Stephen blinked in amazement at his extraordinary caller.

"I appear eminently respectable?"

"Quite. In fact, a most presentable young lady."

"Not so homely, eh?"

"On the contrary, I think most connoisseurs of femininity would regard you as downright beautiful. But I shall not go to dinner with you."

"Why?"

"Well, while the experience might be delightful, I think you're too pert—just a trifle too sure of yourself."

The lovely face drooped sorrowfully. "Oh, Stephen, would you be that mean to poor little Penelope?"

"Good god of love!" Stephen almost yelled. "Are you my little Penelope?"

"Of course I am. Oh, Stephen, you great booby, not to recognize me! You're wearing my watch, too."

He came from behind his desk, took her fiercely by the shoulders and gazed down at her, too amazed to speak. "That's a pretty good second-hand nose, isn't it?" Penelope queried, with just the suspicion of a quaver in her tone. "Don't tell me you disapprove. I adore it myself."

Very soberly he quoted:

"And you, my sweet Penelope, out there
    somewhere you wait for me,
With buds of roses in your hair, and kisses
    on your mouth."

"Oh, Stevie!" she whispered. "Take one."

He took three and hugged her fraternally. "My dear,

dear girl," he declared, "if I were a praying man I'd get right down on my knees and send up a prayer of gratitude to Omnipotence. You're well? You're all well?"

"Oh, yes, indeed I am!" the girl cried with a catch in her voice. "I'm happy—not perfectly happy but— hug me! Oh, Stephen, Stephen, it was so hard not to come back when I received your cablegram. But I had to fight things out and I didn't want to come home until I could meet you bravely. Stephen, are you truly glad to see me again?"

"I am," he answered, and marveled that he should be so glad as he was. His heart, for some mad reason, was singing within him. "Sit down," he commanded, and went back to his own chair. "I'm going to talk to you for five minutes, and then the subject will be taboo forever. Imagine a long hill with a deep pond at the foot of it—a pond all scummy green and slimy —a miasmatic pond. Imagine that you started running down that hill in the dark, that you stubbed your toe and rolled the remainder of the way—into that pond. Well, that's exactly what happened to you. You were running in the dark and you stubbed your toe and landed in a social stratum equivalent to that scummy pond. Do you remember your foster-mother?"

"Faintly—as one remembers faces and events of one's childhood."

"Well, don't bother to remember her. Her cruelty almost ruined your life, but she is out of your life now, never to return. So disabuse your mind of her. There are four human beings living who know that Penelope Gatlin and Nance Belden were one and the same; but those four also know that Nance Belden was a familiar, an unlovely, unwished-for imp that evicted the soul of Penelope Gatlin. I wrote you a meticulous account of your illness, so you understand all about that, but what I want you to know now is that no power on earth can ever discover you for the purpose of making you pay the penalty for the misdeeds of Nance Belden. By the way, where did you get that name?"

"I had forgotten who I was and I had to have a name. So I picked that one out of a book."

"You wandered in amnesia for a long time and you wandered into strange places and met strange people. They are all lost to you. If they met you again they would never recognize you and I doubt if you'd recognize them. They were beyond the social pale, but they were wonderful to you. Whatever they were, they had some fine, godlike attributes and they protected poor little lost you. You never were a bad girl. Nothing could ever make Dan and Lanny and me believe that. So you must not worry and grieve about it. You must forget it. Your cure for that sad memory is not in striving to abstain from thinking about it, but in thinking about it quite clearly and rationally—in facing the horror bravely. The more you do this, the more unimportant it becomes, the more rational and sane it will appear to you to take a philosophical view of the sad experience."

"I have done just that, Stephen. It was so hard at first. I'd shudder when I thought of it. That's why I've been away so long. I had to beat my terrible thoughts, I had to triumph over them. And I have succeeded."

He smiled. "The new nose helped wonderfully, didn't it?"

She nodded. "I do not want to hide from people now, Stephen."

"You must not. That would be depriving the people of the sight of something very sweet and wonderful."

The eager wistfulness in her fine eyes thrilled him. "Do you think I'm sweet and wonderful, Stephen? Lanny does and Dan does, but oh, somehow, I want you to most of all. I want you to be so proud of your handiwork."

"My dear, come here," he commanded, "and sit on my knees just as you used to do when you were Nance Belden and a simple child of impulse—when you hadn't the least compunction about making love to me."

Penelope flushed, but nevertheless obeyed. Stephen placed an arm around her neck and drew her cheek down to his. "I want to tell you something," he murmured. "The first night I saw you, my heart went out to you. And when Dan told me how it all happened, I had a tremendous admiration for your courage and wit. I love brainy people, Penelope, and you have brains. I knew what was wrong with you and I felt so sorry for you, my poor dear; I wanted to help you more than I ever wanted to help any human being. You had a terrible nose, but the eyes and not the nose interested me most. I understood all about you; you were just a little lost atom crying so pitifully to be saved, to know love and protection and happiness, that you developed into a game, and Lanny and Dan and I just had to play it to the finish."

"Have you thought of me sometimes?" she wanted to know.

"Oftener than I cared to admit to myself. Penelope, I know all about you. In this box on my desk are all the records. Look at them, Penelope dear."

"Then you bothered to find out everything—you cared for me just a little bit?"

"A considerable bit—just how much I didn't realize until now. I don't want to let you go, Penelope. I want you for my patient always. I want the job of looking after you."

"What do you mean, Stephen?"

"I'm clumsy, I dare say, but I have more than a suspicion that I've been in love with you—and now that I have you back I'm quite certain I love you enough to want you to marry me. I think my love for you will grow with the years."

"And you'll never think back—never be ashamed of me—never regret your course? And are you sure this isn't just pity?"

"Pity is akin to love. It started in pity, sweetheart —and it's growing every minute. Fast work, my Penelope, but I'm not afraid to trust my instinct. You're my woman. You love me a little, do you not?"

"Why," said Penelope soberly, "I've loved you from the day Dan brought me to this office. You were kind to me, and you didn't seem to see my nose. I was so grateful—and ever since I've been waiting out there, somewhere." She hugged him fiercely. "Oh, Stevie, darling, all the rest of my life I shall devote to you. I'll not be oppressive with my love and I'll not be possessive, but I do want the task of adding to your happiness. I know what happiness is. I can appreciate even a little bit—and I'll never forget to cherish what you give me and give back all I can. We'll be comrades, Stevie."

"That way happiness lies. You seem to have the formula," he replied gravely. "Now, kiss me eight or fifteen or twenty-nine times more and we'll go out to dinner."

The door from Miss Ordway's office opened and the nurse looked in. She flushed as she observed the strange patient in Dr. Burt's arms; seemingly she desired a hole into which she might crawl. However, she had a duty to perform, so she said coldly:

"I'm sorry, Dr. Burt, but Professor Finnegan has just telephoned that you are fifteen minutes late to your engagement to meet the great German savant, Herr Doktor Ufflitz. Professor Finnegan seemed just a trifle annoyed."

"But I didn't press the button, Miss Ordway."

"I know you didn't, Stevie, dear," Penelope spoke up, "but I did—accidentally, with my toe."

"Oh! So that explains the interruption. Miss Ordway, present my compliments to Professor Finnegan and tell him I'd be obliged if he'd drop dead."

Miss Ordway blushingly withdrew.

"Who is Professor Finnegan, darling?" Penelope wanted to know.

"Just a fictitious person Lanny and I invented to help rid me of nuts that stay too long, sweetheart. You don't have to consider him at all."

"I wouldn't, of course," said Penelope.

THE END

CPSIA information can be obtained at www.ICGtesting.com
Printed in the USA
LVOW082037251112

308700LV00005B/559/P